Why
Women
Shouldn't
Marry

Why Women Shouldn't Marry

by Cynthia S. Smith

Lyle Stuart Inc. ✺ *Secaucus, New Jersey*

Published by Lyle Stuart Inc.
120 Enterprise Ave., Secaucus, N.J. 07094
In Canada: Musson Book Company
A division of General Publishing Co. Limited
Don Mills, Ontario

Queries regarding rights and permissions should be
addressed to: Lyle Stuart, 120 Enterprise Avenue
Secaucus, N.J. 07094

Manufactured in the United States of America

Library of Congress Cataloging-in-Publication Data

Smith, Cynthia S.
        Why women shouldn't marry / by Cynthia S. Smith.
        p.   cm.
        ISBN 0-8184-0467-1 : $14.95
        1. Single women--United States. 2. Marriage--United States.
I. Title.
HQ800.2.S65   1988
305.4'890652--dc 19   88-14738
                                                              CIP

To Hillary,
with love and appreciation

Acknowledgments

I WANT TO CONVEY special thanks to the many women who were willing to reveal their life experiences and express their innermost feelings for this book. Their hope, and mine, is that their important contribution will serve to ease the way for every woman who has viewed herself as being alone in the conflict of married vs. single.

My special thanks to my daughter, Hillary, who provided inestimable advice and who alerted my ear to the deeper sounds of truth rather than the hollow sounds of sophistry.

Particular credit must go to my friend and editor, Carole Stuart, who has been a supportive and collaborative force in this project. Her work, from inception of the concept through all stages of the manuscript, has been invaluable.

Contents

tances him professionally. Secure women don't need insecure men. Single is sensational. The tremendous growth of "live-alones" and why. The new awareness of sexual attractiveness after forty, fifty and sixty.

The lovely liberation of living alone. The almost sensuous satisfaction of dining in solitary splendor.

Marriage no longer the only way to live. Couples who live together in single bliss. The pleasures of conjugality with none of the constrictions. "Marriage would change me into someone I don't want to be." Getting married can destroy relationships because of unrealistic expectations. Flexibility, freedom and romance when there's no legal tie.

Not all women want children. The total acceptability of maternity without marriage. New option of single motherhood: cases of happy mothers, happy children and no fathers.

married-never-again" syndrome. Those
who seem to search for husbands but actually prefer the single life.

"Poor old-maid Aunt Martha" who really
had it made. The revisionist view of
unmarried ladies who were not pitifully rejected, but selectively sensibly single.

Financial and legal tips for single women.
How to plan for your future if you are single,
and their future if you are single with children. How to buy a house wisely, alone or
with a live-along. Kinds of insurance you
need. How to protect you and your possessions when you live together and don't
marry: contracts to supplant the marriage
contract. Why you must have a will.

Single by *choice*. Just a statistic, not a life sentence. Put an end to "must marry madness."
Stop looking and start living. Single is successful.

Why
Women
Shouldn't
Marry

Introduction

TODAY THERE ARE ONLY two basic reasons for a woman to marry: sperm and support.

If you need neither of the above, why give up your wonderful freedom, adjust to another person's lifestyle, silence yourself to accommodate to a man's needs, become his domestic slave and emotional caretaker?

Should you want children, then marriage makes sense because a husband furnishes the three F's: fertilization, the fathering figure and financial support. Even here there is an alternate choice. Today marriage is no longer mandatory for motherhood, and many women have opted to go it as single mothers.

But maybe you do not have the primal craving to be a mother. The sacrosanct dogma that all women are born with a powerful maternal instinct and that motherhood is the ultimate female fulfillment is now being refuted as more and more mothers are coming out of the closet to confess that they wish they weren't. You know that another sacred cow has bitten the dust when that major middle America guru Ann Landers devotes a column to the confessions of regretful mothers who write that if they had it to do over, they'd never have children.

If you have been widowed or divorced and already have children what is your incentive to remarry? The famous English mystery story writer P.D. James, who was widowed some years ago, was recently asked by a *People* magazine interviewer whether she intended to marry again. "What for?" was her answer as she went on to say that she had no intention of starting a family as she had three grown children, and that although she enjoyed men for travel, dinner and sex, there was a great pleasure in saying goodbye at the door and returning to the precious privacy of her own home. If you have passed the grief of loss which overcomes widows and divorcees alike, albeit in different ways, you have probably established a highly satisfying existence that is, for the first time in your life, totally devoted to *your* wants and needs. Why on earth should you allow a man to move in on you bringing his demands that force you to reshape your life into his image?

Since the beginning of humankind, women have been driven into marriage by fears of their own inadequacies. We can't take care of ourselves, we can't support ourselves, we need the strength of men to lean upon and control our lives. Men are better and wiser. They're the ones who are destined to run the world. A woman's value is to be judged by the achievements of her husband and thus an unmarried woman is doomed to a diminished and piteous existence.

Then came the women's movement, and women realized that the emperor is wearing no clothes. We learned that, given training and opportunity, women could do everything men had brainwashed us into believing only they could do.

When my husband died, one of my European-born women friends said to me: "Of course, you will marry again."

"Why?" I asked.

"But you must have a man to take care of you," she answered.

Since it had always seemed to me in all the marriages I had observed, as well as mine, that caretaking was the woman's department, I was puzzled.

"What must he take care of?"

She looked at me in total surprise and then answered in her best *"ça va sans dire"* voice:

"Why, of course, to take care of the car, to pay the bills, take care of the money, all those things that men do."

Aha, all that. The sort of things my father handled for fifty-two years and my mother learned to do within two months after he died. The kind of tasks now performed by a large percentage of suburban housewives because their commuting husbands do not have the time. The simple responsibilities assumed by millions of single women as routine chores.

What exactly do men contribute to marriage? Sex and companionship are readily available and socially acceptable without the bonds of matrimony so that's no longer a major draw. Years ago he brought home the bacon and she cooked it, but today she does both equally well.

When researching my book *The Seven Levels Of Marriage; Expectations Vs. Reality*, one of the questions I posed in all male interviews was: "Who do you feel gives the most in your marriage?" Ninety-two percent of men queried answered instantly: "My wife." And frequently gave a figure such as "She's eighty percent and I'm twenty." Or numbers that were equally disparate. Most of the giving and the compromising involved in marriage is performed by the woman. Why do we do it? Is it because we have been socialized to believe that we have more to gain from the arrangement and therefore must suppress our desires and sublimate our needs in order to make HIM happy?

Marriage has usually been regarded in lore and law as a trap for men and a sinecure for woman. Emily Hahn wrote as recently as 1956 that: "Necessity as well as instinct sends the ladies pell-mell to the altar; it is only the secondary things, social pressure or conscience, that sends the men." Women's magazines were filled with instructive articles on "How to catch a husband" or "How to snare a man" always using verbs implying entrapment. It is also true that little girls sit and doodle monograms with the boy-across-the-street's last name after theirs. And there are bride magazines but no groom magazines. That's because we have been conditioned from infancy to regard "making a good marriage" (meaning he's rich or powerful) as the supreme feminine achievement, and the unmarried woman as a publicly branded failure. And a mother whose miserable daughter was married at nineteen to some repellent misfit feels entitled to the smugness of superiority over her friend whose lovely, successful daughter has opted to reject the option of settling for the first available schlep and chooses to wait until she finds a man she really wants to marry.

Today we live in The Age of Iconoclasm created by that wonderful "Why Generation" of the sixties who refused to accept any givens and taught us all to question everything, even such things as American as war and motherhood.

Now you are allowed to wonder "Do I really want to marry and what's in it for me?" without feeling you have committed blasphemy.

It is the time for *choice*. It is time to challenge and cast aside tenets that have crippled us for centuries. The first cliche to go is the antideluvian concept that an unmarried woman is a pathetic spinster while an unmarried man is an enviable bachelor.

OK, they gave us the vote. Slowly, they are inviting us into their boardrooms and private clubs. Now it's time we are accepted into the biggest closed club in history—The Bachelorhood Club. That's the one to which all unmarried non-gay men are automatically admitted: membership conveys the cachet of instant image as suave, swinging socially-in-demand studs and immediate identification with such leering sophistry as George Bernard Shaw's "A married man is a man with a past, while a bachelor is a man with a future." Never mind that the bachelor is a klutzy unappetizing-looking schnook with the personality of a comatose squid. If he isn't married, we must assume it is the choice of the dashing man-about-town who has not yet found any woman wonderful enough to seduce him away from his sybaritic existence.

It's time that unmarried women were given equal status. It's time to recognize that women no longer have to marry to achieve happiness and to *not* be a wife is a viable choice—hers.

That's what this book is about. Why should you marry? What will you really get out of it and what will you give up? Is it worth changing your life, perhaps not for the better, just to acquire the title of "Mrs." which many women have dropped in favor of "Ms." Once you begin to weigh the compensations against the concessions, the bonds of matrimony may get to look more constrictive than constructive.

There are millions of women today who are making the decision to stay single and love it. I went around the country interviewing such women and their stories may match yours. It's time to stop the pursuit of a cliche existence merely because your mother and friends expect it and to rethink *your* choice of lifestyle. Why should you go through the demeaning hassles of dealing with frightened men who twist themselves and you into neurotic pretzels just to avoid "commitment"? Who needs them and who needs marriage? Maybe not you.

I'm Thirty-Eight and Not Married. How Did This Happen?

Life does not give itself to one who tried to keep all its advantages at once. I have often thought morality may perhaps consist solely in the courage of making a choice.
—LEON BLUM (on marriage)

"I ALWAYS THOUGHT I'd be married by this time with a house and kids. What happened?"

This question is being posed by millions of women between the ages of thirty and forty-four who are puzzled to find themselves in lifestyle positions they had never envisioned. They followed the new rules for women's self-fulfillment and went on to become whatever their abilities permitted, the first generation to be freed of the constrictions of career gender discrimination and the rigid role assignments in male/female relations. Instead of serving the roast chicken dinner they slaved over all day and listening enviously to their husbands' dinnertime tales of stimulating activities in the boardrooms or courtrooms as their mothers did, today's women are participants rather than spectators in the exciting worlds of business, professions and government. They are not relegated to the kitchen but are movers and shakers who have the great satisfaction of using their brains and talents to affect the world at large rather than the small arenas of home and local community to which women had traditionally been restricted. They love it, they enjoy their work and revel in their achievements, but deep down there's a little piece of them that wants to cook and serve that roast chicken.

The problem is, to whom?

What happened to the men between thirty and forty-four who should have been husbands and fathers? They are still little boys playing aimlessly with their electronic toys and living in a state of perpetual adolescence, afraid to grow up and take on the responsibilities their fathers assumed unquestioningly.

The cover story of *The New York Times Magazine* of November 15, 1987, titled "Why Wed? The Ambivalent American Bachelor," portrayed a series of men in their thirties and forties who are part of the 13.8 percent of thirty-to-forty-four-year-old men the current

United States Census Bureau reports as never married. As one of the men said:

"I think I was an adolescent all through my thirties," and describes how a woman left him after a six-year relationship because he could not commit to marriage. "I could not marry her because I had not grown up."

Hot flash! The whole fuss about the inability of today's men to grow up is laughable to women who have always known that fact. As one married woman put it, "The only one of your children who does not grow up and move away is your husband."

Every woman who has lived with a man has seen the child-side that is part of him forever and has found this aspect alternately annoying and endearing. But under the eternal Women's Rules of Male/Female Interaction that dictate the importance of never allowing him to see any signs of her superiority for fear he'll feel threatened, women have hidden their greater maturity and continued the pretense that men are the stronger sex.

Little girls mature far faster than little boys, a fact that's obvious at the grade school level. At least we used to be able to expect that the boys would catch up eventually, but not any more.

The Bachelor as a Jerk

The *Times* article went on to point out that the public attitude toward bachelors is quite different than it was years ago and "The very word 'bachelor,' which once evoked a 1930's Cary Grant figure—irresistible to women but ultimately unconquerable—is now dated. . . . The 1980's are the years of the bachelor, not as a debonair hero, but to put it as bluntly as some women do, the bachelor as a jerk."

The dictionary defines the word jerk as "dull, fatuous, stupid, numbskull," which must be viewed as an acceptable description of men who spend their lives avoiding commitment to comfort, convenience and the nurturing supplied by wives. The bachelors interviewed for the *Times* article conveyed a mixed bag of fears: fear of commitment, fear of marriage, fear of yielding self, fear of giving up dreams, fear of growing up. But the real fear that paralyzes such men was never mentioned—the fear of being found wanting. And with good reason.

In their book *Why Can't Men Open Up?*, Steven Naifeh and Gregory White Smith tell women how to cope with these new male conflicts (if they think it's worth the bother, parenthetical comment is mine):

"A woman must distance herself from her man's problems instead of seeing his struggling as a rejection of her. She must see him as a flawed individual who needs her strength and tenderness."

Never before has a generation of men been faced with such a challenge to their sense of adequacy and masculinity. Raised by doting mothers to be the stalwart providers who would be desired and accepted by compliant women, they reached marriageable age in a new era of independent achieving women who demand equitable partnership status in marriage rather than the old lord-and-master-of-the-house setup. Like victims of the technological revolution, these men were trained for jobs that have suddenly been eliminated. Now instead of seeing marriage as a way to assert superiority, they view it as a route to dependency.

In her book *The Hearts of Men; American Dreams and the Flight from Commitment*, the social historian Barbara Ehrenreich points out the ambivalence that makes men yearn for the security of a loving relationship but fear its segue into dependency.

"He loves the early stages—he opens up, delighted to find the relationship he longs for. But the very fulfillment evokes deep-seated fears of dependency and vulnerability."

The beginning of a relationship fills him with ego-building notions of male success with women, but then he quickly becomes terrified of becoming engulfed. He gets hostile, feels trapped and begins to retreat. The transition from attraction to withdrawal is really a manifestation of his fear of dependency which men equate with weakness.

What crippled this generation of men even further was the counterculture of the 1960's which eschewed the conformity of marriage, followed by the 1970's California-created drive for self-fulfillment that locked them into permanent adolescence. In his 1970 book *The Greening of America*, Charles Reich notes:

"Marriage meant being 'adult' which meant no more hope of excitement, no more fun, a sudden and final leap into middle age."

The February 28, 1988, *New York Times Magazine* column called "About Men" was written by a young man who has just reached the age of twenty-six and is questioning whether or not he is an adult, and does he really want to be. He mentions that he does not have any health insurance or credit cards. He speaks of his girlfriend from high school days three years older than he who is now a highly paid lawyer and whose last year's raise was more than he had earned in the entire year. He points out that she has insurance and credit cards and is thus deprived of the wonderful freedom of not needing money. Maybe because she's been picking up the dinner checks?

Could you ever have imagined seeing an article like that in the 1940's or fifties? Any man of twenty-six (and they were men then) would have been embarrassed to admit to such immaturity and would have viewed such an article as a confession of failure rather than a vehicle for proud public catharsis.

A Generation of Peter Pans

So we have a marvelous generation of mature achieving women coupled with a peer group of men who are Peter Pans. The reason that so many thirty-to-forty-four-year-old women have not married is they realized along the way, as they met and had relationships with these men, that the promised benefits of matrimony were illusionary because the mature, responsible and loving life partners they were seeking were non-existent. Maybe they always were, but previous generations of women were ill-equipped to quibble, so they compromised, they played dumb, they accepted the trade-offs. Because they had no choice.

Today's woman has a *choice*. She does not have to consign herself to sharing her life and building a home with a man she may not respect or care for deeply, a mate who cannot provide her with the emotional satisfactions she needs. The time has come to view marriage not as a rite de passage but as a right of choice.

Certainly there are millions of happy marriages that work out fine for both partners. People are still getting married every day. I was very happily married for 35 years but I was in the no-choice era where only oddballs and rejects were unmarried. I made a large number of compromises and did a lot of game-playing to maintain the mandatory socially acceptable facade of male supremacy. I was willing to do this because I didn't grow up with MS. magazine but with *Ladies' Home Journal* in the days when women were evaluated not by what they did but by what they cooked. I enjoyed being married and was willing to accept the trade-offs. My marriage was a product of the times, just as being unmarried is a product of today's times.

A 1985 study of trends undertaken for *Cosmopolitan* magazine by Battelle Memorial Institute's research center in Seattle concluded that marriage has become less central to women's lives. The Census Bureau statistics indicate the percentage of women ages twenty-five to thirty-four who have never married has more than doubled since 1970. This is because women are not only postponing marriage, say the authors of the *Cosmo* study as reported in the October 12, 1987, issue of *Time*, but increasingly avoiding it. "The old economic division of labor in which men work outside the home while women provide what economists call 'home production'—cooking, caring for children and so on—is gone, and thus the 'gains from marriage for women have declined.' "

A report in the *Journal of Marriage and the Family* comparing 15 years of data compiled by the University of Chicago's National Opinion Research Center concludes that marriage in the U.S. is a "weakened and declining institution," primarily because women are getting less out of it. The authors, Sociologist Norval Glenn of the University of Texas at Austin and Charles Weaver of St. Mary's University of San Antonio, have found that women are less happy in marriage today than in the past, probably because having a husband now means an increased load of responsibilities rather than the traditional trade-off of homemaking for financial support.

Here we are, twenty-five years after Betty Friedan's revolutionary book *The Feminine Mystique*, and the front page of *The New York Times* reports the result of a nation-wide survey of 1,870 people conducted between October 29 and November 5, 1987, which shows that "even though more women are in the work force, they are still the primary care-givers and the people who pay attention to how, when, what and where the families eat . . . and that the idea of equality in the home is an illusion."

Ninety-one percent of the married women who participated in the survey said they do the shopping and employment outside of the home did not free them; 90 percent of the married women who work full time do the primary shopping for their families, as well as most or all of the cooking. According to Ann Weber, a social psychologist and an associate professor at the University of North Carolina at Asheville: "Women feel bad if they don't do what is expected of them, and men think they have a right to expect it. It will take a lot longer than a couple of decades to see changes."

"After centuries of clearly defined roles for men and women, a couple of decades is not enough to make a difference," said Dr. Joseph Pleck, the Luce Professor of the Family at Wheaton College in Norton, Mass. "The family as an institution changes rather slowly. Men's participation is increasing, but it's got a long way to go."

Where does that leave women today? Years ago when most women did not work and we subscribed to the breadwinner ethic there was a fair and equitable quid pro quo. Of course, marriage is not to be regarded as merely a business arrangement but involves fulfillments and soul-enriching benefits that cannot be measured on a scale like so many apples and potatoes. But a certain balance should be expected. Eliminating the emotional factors, when today's man marries he gets a home, a housekeeper, a cook, a cheering squad and another paycheck. When a woman marries, she gets a boarder.

Is this fair? Of course not, yet the old ball-and-chain myth that purports marriage as an institution created for the benefit and protection of women continues. The reality of the husband/wife positions is quite different. Every wife I interviewed cited the almost total inability of her husband to function in the home without her.

"When I get sick, my husband is not only useless, he's irritable. He never thinks of even bringing me a cup of tea. But when he gets sick, he expects me to wait on him hand and foot."

When a husband goes away on a trip, he just takes clean socks, shirts and underwear out of the drawers where his wife has placed them, tosses them into his case and is off. When a wife goes away for any more than one day, she loads the freezer with packages marked "Reheat at 350° for fifteen minutes," fills the fridge with goodies, leaves notes about where to find things, checks the toilet paper supply and then departs in a state of exhaustion from tending to last minute details knowing that she will return to a house that will look and smell like the locker room of a Central American soccer team.

In Josephine Tey's *The Franchise Affair*, the charming fortyish lawyer is stunned to have his proposal of marriage turned down by the fortyish woman he has successfully defended. When he warns her that it could be a lonely life, she answers:

"A 'full' life in my experience is usually full only of other people's demands."

The irony of the perpetual adolescent generation of men who are busy avoiding marriage is they are depriving themselves of these marvelous caretaking services and nurturing of women who historically are the homemakers to whom all roamers yearn to return. Ulysses kept himself going with the image of faithful Penelope who was keeping the home fires burning. Country-Western music is filled with songs chronicling the willful wanderings of men who drink themselves to sleep at night in faroff places with their guitars and fond memories of wives and mothers patiently awaiting their men's return home.

Perhaps what is really deterring men from taking the nuptial step is not so much fear of commitment as fear of failure. They are concerned about their abilities to perform successfully as husbands and fathers. It's not unlike being loath to risk applying for an important job for fear of rejection, it's less ego-threatening to fool yourself that you really don't want that job anyway. Today's generation of women is hot stuff, they're solid, talented, achieving, responsible, independent. What can these admittedly immature men offer such women?

The New Breed of Woman

The February 23, 1988, issue of *The Examiner* is headed "Hollywood's Glamorous Spinsters" and shows five famous and glamorous women who have opted to remain unmarried.

"At forty-four, Donna Mills has her own Beverly Hills mansion, a thriving career, and no desire to turn her live-in lover record producer Richard Holland, into her husband.

" 'I don't need a spouse to pay the bills,' she says. 'I can pay them myself, the way I've always done.' And the Knots' Landing temptress has no dreams of becoming a mom, either. She's not the maternal type and doesn't want to change her life in midstream.

" 'I never wanted a husband or children,' she told a reporter. 'And I don't need the marriage ceremony to make me feel more complete as a human being. I'm quite content being single.' "

Apparently the gorgeous Jacqueline Bisset has the same feelings about matrimony. She has been living with Russian ballet star Alexander Godunov for the past six years, but at forty-three, she still considers marriage out of the question.

Diane Keaton says she loves being single and the forty-one-year-old actress lives all alone in a beautiful New York apartment and has no wish to share it with a husband. She has had a series of relationships with famous men like Woody Allen and Warren Beatty, but marriage has so far not occurred.

TV star Tracy Scoggins at age twenty-nine is happy to share her luxurious home with five cats and her sixty-seven-year-old mother. She claims that she doesn't need a man to look after her, she earns her own money and runs her own life, so "What's the point of getting married? I'm perfectly happy the way I am—single!"

One forty-two-year-old woman I interviewed for this book told me that she would like to find "a man who is important to my life" but saw no reason to change her single way of living for anything less. Men need women and women need men, not just for sex but for the complementary qualities they supply for each other. But we no longer live in a "couples world" and women are now free to enjoy male/female relationships without the need for legal or binding attachments.

The divorce rate in the United States is holding fairly close to 50 percent which tells us that marriage is not for everyone, and that half the people find it an acceptable way to live but the other half does not.

Whichever half you are in is strictly up to you. Today, it's your choice.

◆§ TWO §◆

"Who Needs a He When I Have Me?"

Who is it that says most? which can say
  more
Than this rich phrase—that you alone
  are you?
  —WILLIAM SHAKESPEARE, Sonnet 84

ALICE HUNG UP the phone and her friend Mary, noting the familiar look of sorrow and anger, said:
  "Not another of those 'we'd-better-stop-seeing-each-other-because-I'm-getting-to-like-you-too-much-and-you-might-want-to-get-married' calls?"

Alice nodded, flopped into a chair and said disgustedly:

"What makes that yo-yo think I want to marry him, or anybody for that matter?"

If a young woman said that forty years ago, the statement would have been regarded as either sour grapes or stupidity. Which girl didn't want to become "Mrs." and have a husband, home and family . . . live in the style his hopefully growing ambition and income would provide and be secure in the knowledge that she would be taken care of for the rest of her life? How else could a woman's success be measured? If she was unfortunate enough to remain unmarried, it was universally accepted that this was not out of choice but because she was unlovable and unlovely, or the victim of a tragic love affair.

Over half of the unmarried lady teachers in my high school were rumored to have suffered the losses of sweethearts in "The War." We never knew who spread the rumors, but I suspect they themselves did in order to convey an image of romance rather than rejection and to mitigate the ugly epithet of "old maid."

The New
"Old Maid"

You would be hard-pressed to reconcile the cliché image of an "old maid" with thirty-eight-year-old Alice. Instead of Enna Jettick shoes and shapeless

print dresses, she wears Reeboks and jeans. Any re-
semblance to the prim crimped and colorless spinster
of yore is quickly forgotten when you see this trim,
blond and extremely attractive woman who exudes
vitality.

Alice grew up in a middle-class home in a suburb
of a major city, the only child of intelligent, loving but
not overly indulgent parents. She went off to college
for a Fine Arts degree and returned home until she
found a job in her chosen field of communications,
whereupon she moved into her own apartment.

"I love my job and my life. I have lots of friends,
men and women; there's always lots to do and people
to do it with. Sure, I sort of expect to get married
someday, but that so-called right someone just hasn't
materialized. Maybe because I don't need a husband
the way women did years ago. I've been moving
along in my career, making more and more money
and getting a big kick out of spending it freely. I've
enjoyed furnishing my apartment just the way I
liked. I hear married friends of mine arguing with
husbands over every stick of furniture—she likes it,
he doesn't. She buys it and he shrieks at the price . . .
it becomes a major hassle. I've picked out every piece
carefully, it's my home, my taste and I love it. And I
buy clothes whenever I want without having to jus-
tify the bills to anyone. I'm free to travel on my own,
unencumbered by the pulls of a partner. I go when I
want and where I want. I'm totally free and it's un-
beatable. I have nothing against marriage, but as I see
it now, how will it improve my life?"

Alice has had a number of relationships over the

years and each time there was a possibility of culmination in marriage that just never worked out. The
most recent one was with Tom, an accountant with
whom Alice was deeply in love.

At first, they saw each other constantly until it
seemed to make sense to live together. Since Alice
had the larger apartment, Tom moved in. The first six
months were heavenly. Tom had a good job with a
large accounting firm and Alice was happy in her position. They enjoyed cooking dinner together, shopping together, jogging, playing tennis and meeting
with friends. Tom was loving and caring and romantic. From time to time, he would surprise her with little gifts and Alice's feeling for him was becoming
deeper and deeper. The strong sexual passion of their
relationship was developing into something warm
and wonderful as each cared and learned to please
the other.

Then one day Alice received a call at her office
from a former employer offering her the position as
head of the city's cultural arts center, a job that would
offer not only tremendous responsibility and salary
increase, but high public visibility and the chance to
become part of the top echelon of movers and shakers
in the community. It was the opportunity of a lifetime
and she couldn't wait to get home to share her wonderful news with Tom and talk over the myriad ways
this new career could change their lives. She found
him in the kitchen. Their agreed routine was that
whoever got home first started dinner. Alice tossed
down her bag and attache case and without even
stopping to remove her coat gave him a big hello kiss

and began to regale him with the details of the phone call and the job offer.

"Imagine! I am going to be the administrator of all the arts activities in this city! I'll be responsible for the coordination of the ballet, symphony and opera performances at the Fine Arts Center . . . that means booking performers, arranging for funding, working with the producers, directors and artists . . ." her voice trailed off as she suddenly realized that Tom had not said one word or registered any response to her enthusiastic outpouring but merely continued to chop and slice onions, mushrooms and other ingredients for a stir fry dinner.

"Don't you think it's a fantastic opportunity?" she asked somewhat tentatively.

"Sure," he said, "if you like to be an ass-licking whore to a bunch of rich people. All you'll really be is a glorified fund-raiser sucking up to the town muckamucks for contributions. What's the big deal?" Then he moved past her to open the refrigerator where he began rummaging through the shelves.

Alice felt as though she had been kicked in the stomach. In one cruel blow he had managed to douse her enthusiasm and strip her self esteem. How can one human being be so hurtful to another, let alone to someone you profess to love? Here she was proud of being offered what she saw as a dream job and thrilled with the ramifications it promised, and he made her feel like an inept unperceptive idiot. Even if he thought that she was over-reacting to the possibilities the position promised and endowing it with unrealistic advantages, wouldn't it have been kinder to initially respond to her exultation with congratulations and then follow up later with a reasonable discussion? As she went into the bedroom to change into her evening outfit of jeans and T-shirt, her eyes filled with tears. She was devastated as she began to question a future with a man with whom she would now hesitate to share feelings for fear he would savage them. Alice realized that perhaps Tom was either envious or in some way threatened by this change in her career status. She longed to talk it out with him, but was put off by his closed silent face at dinner followed by his refusal to look up from the TV football game for the rest of the evening. She resented that he deprived her of the tremendous pleasure of anticipating the joys the new job promised.

So she did what she had always done before she met Tom: she called her friend Mary and enjoyed an hour phone chat and Mary's screams of delight as they talked about the wonderful people she would be meeting, the parties she would be attending, the fun of leaving the dull world of commerce and entering the thrilling world of the arts. Mary pointed out how this upward move placed Alice in a new higher career level that would insure her future and would surely result in superb peripheral benefits and job offers. It was the kind of conversation that Alice had hoped and expected to have with Tom.

The ensuing months were filled with exciting events and immersion in a totally new world of artists, performers, civic leaders and officials in which Alice was accepted as a respected peer. Work was delightful but home was hell. The reasons for Tom's ini-

tial reaction became obvious as his jealousy mani-
fested itself in offensive and petty ways. His
resentment at her rise resulted in a constant stream of
snide remarks about her being nothing but a foolish
foil for the tax-saving efforts of the rich. It was true
that part of Alice's job consisted of fund-raising
which required attending many charity balls and
large parties in order to mingle with the moneyed
people who could give large donations to the symphony, opera, ballet and museums. To an attractive,
vivacious woman like Alice, this was one of the big
pluses of her position and she hated Tom's trying to
diminish her enjoyment by twisting these gala activities into demeaning money-grubbing chores. She
knew what devils drove him to take this tack, but
knowledge did not make his relentless criticism any
more palatable.

Alice tried to talk with him about his feelings, to
make him see the reasons behind his heinous behavior. But he was impossible to reach. Whenever she
tried to engage him in a discussion, he aborted the effort abruptly with the usual male evasion tactic:

"You're always nagging at me. OK, I'm wrong
and you're right. So what's the point of talking?" and
then he would walk out of the room. It was infuriat-
ing and made her feel totally helpless.

Like many men, Tom had great difficulty in talking about his feelings or trying to understand what
was going on in a relationship. The first page in Shere
Hite's book *Women in Love* begins with "Men's emotional withholding and distancing: reluctance to talk
about personal thoughts and feelings . . . 98 percent

of the women in this study say they would like more verbal closeness with the men they love; they want the men in their lives to talk more about their own personal thoughts, feelings, plans, and questions, and to ask them about theirs." And in their book *Why Can't Men Open Up?* authors Steven Naifeh and Gregory White Smith convey the message: "We're raised to be closed men. By closing ourselves to feelings, we thought we could escape the anxieties and disappointments of emotional involvement."

Alice tried to think how she would feel if Tom outdistanced her professionally. Would she be as jealous and odious? She concluded that she might feel a stab of envy here and there, but on the whole she would be happy for and proud of him. Traditionally, men have been burdened with the emotional baggage of needing to be the superior performer of the household. As Tevya in *Fiddler on the Roof* kept reiterating "But I am the *man* of the house. I make the decisions."

Tom professed to be a modern man who viewed women as equals, and he was fine as long as Alice was equal. What he couldn't accept was when she became more than equal. Like many who view themselves as liberal antitheses to male chauvinists, he is comfortable until challenged by the reality of being surpassed by a woman whereupon the old lord-and-master-syndrome emerges to the horror and disbelief of all concerned.

Tom's anger began to surface alarmingly in the form of irate phone calls to Alice's office when she worked late, and rude demands of her secretary to locate Alice immediately whenever he wanted to discuss some minor matter. His harassing behavior became insufferable and unsupportable and Alice found herself constantly agitated.

Many evenings she would arrive home exhausted and want nothing more than to eat a quiet dinner, watch TV and go to bed. Those times, and there were many, she did not want to deal with anyone, or even talk on the phone. She longed for privacy and solitude. Instead she would be met by a hostile Tom who demanded to be told what had occurred during her day so that he could point out what she had done wrong and disparage her performance and position.

Finally, one day after a particularly brutal confrontation, Alice asked herself "What do I need this for? What am I getting out of this relationship except aggravation?" She loved her job and the new world in which she had become a respected participant. She realized that much of the potential pleasure she could be enjoying was being diminished by the need to pussyfoot around Tom's sensitive psyche. She became aware that his constant emotional abuse had changed their relationship, killed her feelings for him and made living together a misery. She no longer loved him or even liked him. So she told him to leave.

Emotional Shortchanging

Alice had discovered a fact that women have come to realize: true exchange of feelings and emotions come mostly from women friends. Lucky is the gal who can look to her lover or husband for the acknowledgement of problems and intimate talks. All too often men view women as sounding boards for *their* ideas and anxieties but are unwilling to return the favor.

"Afraid like Ulysses, to be lured by the Sirens and yield his freedom, strength and masculinity,"* men are bred to view feelings as feminine and silence as strength. "Torn between the demands of manhood and the need for intimacy, they secretly long for the security of emotional dependence" but are unable to participate in the exchange required of such relationships.

The actress Glenn Close, in discussing the public's reaction to her movie *Fatal Attraction* with *Time* magazine said "the whole male-female thing in this country is very volatile right now. I think many women are feeling used by men. They invest a lot in a relationship, in nurturing a man emotionally and in his career, but they have their own careers and emotions and they don't get nurturing in return." Ms. Close and the man in her life were at the time expecting their first child shortly and had no plans to marry.

Women of past generations accepted being emotionally shortchanged in marriage; they viewed such deprivation as a tradeoff for support and status. But today's women, like Alice, need neither. Their financial condition is securely in their hands, so fiscal dependency is unnecessary. And status? Today, single is sensational. In fact, it's "in."

*Why Can't Men Open Up? Steven Naifeh and Gregory White Smith. New York: Clarkson N. Potter, Inc.

Witness a *U.S. News & World Report* cover story entitled "Living Alone and Learning to Love It" illustrated with a photo of a glamorous thirty-ish to forty-ish woman in a red satin nightgown on a designer-coverleted three thousand dollar brass bed with a book, champagne-and-caviar-filled bedtray and Siamese cat. "More women are putting off marriage in favor of careers. . . . As job opportunities have broadened and incomes risen, baby-boomers in particular have developed a yen to choose the good life alone without support—or interference—from home.

" 'Among the young never-married, the story to be told is the rise of the primary individual,' comments Steven McLaughlin, a population expert at the Battelle Human Affairs Research Centers in Seattle. 'Decisions about lifestyle are no longer controlled by family.'

"The number of live-alones in this group age twenty-five to thirty-four increased by 346 percent between 1970 and 1986. The thirty-five to forty-four age group grew by 258 percent." The story goes on to say that today, society gives singles the nod. "In one generation," says University of Miami sociologist Aaron Lipman, "we've seen singles bars and apartment complexes and vacations and frozen dinners and soups for one." Pillsbury and Sara Lee are doing wonderfully with their pint-sized individual cakes, microwaveable in minutes. Home builders find that singles account for a fourth of first-time home buyers. As the article concludes, "As America's singles find strength in numbers, society is granting them more respect."

To further prove the point, the "Home" section

of *The New York Times* recently depicted three couples who spend Christmas in their summer homes; the lead twosome pictured on the front page was unmarried and had apparently been so for over ten years. When a staid institution like the venerable *Times* equates Mr. & Mrs. couples with a Ms. & Mr. livetogether, you know that singleness is socially acceptable.

"My mother used to nag me to settle down and marry," said Alice, "but now she sees how exciting and fulfilling my life is and admits maybe she's a bit envious. She's spent her life tied to the house and the needs of my father—he did what he wanted and she did what he wanted. I do what I want."

I can hear readers saying to themselves right about here: "Sure she's having a great time. She's pretty, only in her thirties and still attractive to men. But what's going to happen when she hits fifty . . . how great will her life be then?"

Age Is No Longer Crucial

Nothing need change because times have changed and perceptions of beauty and maturity have changed. No longer is a woman regarded as "over the hill" at forty. Role models for sexy ladies have become Jane Fonda, Joan Collins, Linda Evans, Farah Fawcett . . . all long past the flush of youth. Back in the thirties, an actress would have burned her sables rather than admit to a fortieth birthday. In fact, most of them lingered on twenty-nine for as long as cosmetic surgery would permit. When Gloria Steinem turned forty, someone said to her: "My God, you don't look forty," to which she answered, "This is what forty looks like."

Today, age is no longer the gauge of attractiveness or a deterrent to sexual and social activity. Where it would have been regarded as unseemly for an older woman to date (if she was a widow, her children would have been mortified) today's single women of all ages go off on weekends with men friends (and register under their own names, no five-and-ten gold bands required) and in fact, have a series of relationships (which used to be called "affairs" and were discussed only in deliciously scandalized whispers, not in front of the children, of course). Life and love go on right up until death does its part. Florida is filled with men and women in their sixties, seventies and eighties who date, dance and sleep around. They talk about sex with the same horniness as their grandchildren. In fact, conversations I've overheard among some sexy seniors sounded remarkably similar to those in any high school locker room.

Today, maturity is fashionable in both women and men and age is no longer seen to dim allure. Young men find older women attractive as indeed they are, which has served to increase the supply side of suitors for all women. Single and sixty can now mean rock-and-roll rather than the rocking chair. According to Shere Hite, women of all ages find new lovers and new relationships "though many, it turns

out, are not interested in marriage and prefer to remain single." In one case history, she cites a woman
who claims that "I feel good about the way I look. It is
easy to meet someone I like and am attracted to. They
are usually much younger. I'm sixty-three and they
are usually thirty-four to forty-five."

The disparity between their ages may seem
extreme, although not if it occurred the other way
around with the man being thirty years older. An old
guy with a young chick, that's supposed to be. But
many of life's "supposed-to-be's" have been cast
aside these days thanks to the devout iconoclasm of
what I call the "Why Generation"—that great sixties
bunch who changed our accepted ways of living with
one simple word "Why?" It's amazing how easily
time-honored traditions and patterns of behavior can
be withered by the simple method of questioning
their validity.

Years ago, if a forty-two-year-old mother wanted
to go back to college she would have been told the
idea was ridiculous and would never have thought to
ask "why?" As a result of today's questioning the givens, older women have gone back to school and back
into the workforce which has given both those areas a
new heterogeneity that seems perfectly natural. For
perhaps the first time, young men are working with
older women in peer situations and can perceive
them as people rather than as mothers or teachers
which was the only context they had dealt with them
in the past. Young men are being exposed to the
charms and sexual attractiveness of women of all ages
and are reacting normally, like falling in love. Unbur-

dened by the man-must-be-older rule in relationships that has been accepted for centuries, they are choosing women solely by desirability rather than age. Like so many a time-honored customs, current evaluation and examination indicate that it's time to stop honoring it because the cause for its creation is gone.

Why was it always expected that a woman would marry a man older than she? Because historically man was the breadwinner and woman the homemaker and a man did not marry until he was financially secure and able to support a wife and family. Since women were ready for childbearing in their teens and men not established until their twenties and often thirties, she married someone older for security and he married someone younger for fecundity.

Let's not forget that women were, until fairly recently, regarded as lesser than men in the brain department. In 1859, in his book *The Ordeal of Richard Feverel*, George Meredith wrote "I expect that Woman will be the last thing civilized by Man." They didn't let us near the ballot box until 1920. What did a mere woman know about politics, government, law, finance, business, life? She needed a man to "take care of her." Like Nora in Ibsen's *A Doll's House*, she was to be treated like a child with her life controlled totally by her husband/father. Building on this initial assumption that women are inept idiots who need the strong guidance of male competence, women have always coupled with older men. The difference could be five years or fifteen years; any disparity is considered respectable as long as he has the seniority.

But along comes the "Why Generation" who have made all kinds of history by refusing to accept any tradition or convention without a sensible rationale, case by case. We made a war and the young men refused to attend. We tell the young women that it's customary to date older men, and they want reasons for the restriction. Today's woman is a lawyer, executive, welder, policewoman, banker, executive or business owner who is making a solid living and handling the details of her own life capably without the aid of male management. She no longer has to depend on a man for security, so why does he have to be "established," "settled," and older? Will this seniority insure his greater stability or sense? Of course not. In the first place, wisdom does not come with age, only experience does. If a man is not overly bright at twenty, he is not going to blossom into brilliance at forty. Why assume that older means wiser? And second place, even if it did, who needs it? If someone is looking for a sage, superior mate, that someone could just as well be the man as well as the woman. Where is it written that the woman must look up to the man? And that goes literally as well as figuratively. Why should the man always have to be taller? Why is it that when a six-foot male dates a five-foot female, it's acceptable, even adorable. But when a short man and a tall woman fall in love, it is considered comical. If you stop to think about it, isn't this perception just an extension of the conception that big daddy must take care of the little helpless woman and anything else is an aberration?

Today's woman sees no reason to restrict her social relationships by age and feels totally free to explore the attractions of younger as well as older men since she no longer has to depend upon a man for support and security.

And now we come to sexual attractiveness. A woman in her thirties is at her peak of loveliness. In her forties, she has ripened into a mature beauty. At fifty, she can be luscious and in her sixties have an aura of elegant sensuality.

Look at Mary Tyler Moore, long regarded as one of America's darlings. At forty-five she married a twenty-nine-year-old man and years later is still blissfully happy. With Mary as a role model, how can it be wrong? It has always been perfectly acceptable for a rich, famous man to cavort with young beautiful women. He's attracted to their looks and they're turned on by his power. With today's open equality of the sexes, flip the roles and it still works. A rich and famous woman can attract a young handsome man. If both their needs are being met, then it's right. Carly Simon at age forty-one had a boyfriend of thirty. Olivia Newton-John, thirty-eight has a twenty-eight-year-old husband. Bette Midler is married to a younger man. As are Raquel Welch, Arlene Dahl and scores of other famous women.

But it's not only the rich and famous who have reversed the sex roles in May/December relationships as indicated by the woman who responded to Shere Hite's questionnaire and by this column that appeared in the Miami *Herald* last year.

Commenting on an earlier column about women dating younger men, a woman from California wrote:

"I was seventy last July. My husband of forty years died five years ago. I have a fifty-seven-year-old lover. On Sundays, a sixty-one-year-old man takes me to breakfast and to church services. I have to keep him in his place. My thirty-two-year-old income-tax man approached me for a date and I had to refuse because of his obvious intentions." The columnist responded in print: "You certainly have found a solution to the problem of 'there are no men of my age around.' My guess is that you are communicating a youthfulness and vitality that, along with the maturity of your years, makes for a very attractive combination to many men."

Being single at fifty is no less interesting than being single at thirty. You have the same freedom of choice and activities and can have a wonderful exciting life or a comfortably quiet one according to your own preference.

* * *

Lil is a tall, rangy fifty-two-year-old woman whose flowing grey-flecked black hair, large blue unmade-up eyes, defined cheekbones and uncalculatedly casual clothes convey an attractiveness that defies the conventional standards of prettiness.

An art major in college set her off on a varied career that has included establishing her own art gallery which she eventually sold, acting as curator for a private art collector, running a shop that sold artifacts. At this point in her life, she has become a private consultant to corporate art purchasers and commutes be-

tween London and New York where she lives in an
apartment that is cluttered with paintings and sculp-
ture and two Siamese cats who thread their way
adroitly through pre-Columbian art pieces and can-
vasses that are stacked up on the floor against chairs
and tables. She paints, and continues to sell her
paintings as well as those of other artists.

Lil was married at age thirty-two for three years
to a charming man who was twenty years older than
she and with whom she had lived for two years. The
marriage was something she did not want, but was
the result of parental pressure from, as Lil describes
her, "a Victorian southern belle mother who finally
got to me."

"I have never wanted to have children, so why
on earth did I get married? After three years together,
I found myself bored, restless and wondering what I
was doing there. I couldn't see myself building a future with him, so I left."

"My relationships last three years," she said
matter-of-factly. "It has become a pattern in my life.
The first two years are romantic and exciting, but
then I find I have to put so much energy and time into
the relationship that my work begins to suffer . . . it
takes too much out of me and there's no 'me' any
more. I resent that. Also, I don't like being perceived
as a 'couple'—it's a whole different thing and you
lose your individuality. That's how you're seen when
you are married. You are lumped together into a take-
it-or-leave-it twosome. 'Love her, hate him so let's
forget them both'—who wants that? My mother used
to insist that I need a man to take care of me. What

for? I have an assistant who pays my bills and an accountant who takes care of my income tax."

Lil has had a series of relationships—some of them sexual and some of them platonic.

"I have a wonderful male friend in London now. He's an absolutely delightful escort and friend . . . we go to theatre, visit his friends, go out for dinner. We enjoy each other tremendously. But we have both deliberately avoided sex because that changes the entire configuration of a relationship. I would never think of living with him, either, because it would be disaster. He's a real super-fastidious Mr. Tidy and as you can see from my apartment, I'll never get the *House Beautiful* award.

"In fact, I have never met any man I would want to spend my life with. Obviously it works for some people, there are lots of women who are happily married or have long-term serious intimate relationships. But for me, the thought of spending every day forever with the same person is horrifying. It just would never work for me. There are some dependent kind of women who need to be with someone all the time, who just can't seem to be by themselves. There are actually women who have asked me how to be alone, for God's sakes. I ask them how they can be with someone they don't like. There are men who can't be alone either. One guy I know buys two tickets night after night for different activities. He's terrified of being alone . . . it's as though it brands him a social failure. He just cannot face being by himself. But if you met him, you wouldn't want to be with him, either. He's an inane twit with the inner resources of a snail.

"I see no marriage among my friends that I would want. In fact, I see married friends living in intolerable situations. I spent Thanksgiving with a couple—it was a horror. She gave up her career as an editor fifteen years ago because she wanted a family. She married this man who treats her absolutely sadistically. He storms around the house, is always in a fury of some sort over some minor infraction, he's demanding and demeans her constantly. They have a child, poor thing, who's been in therapy for years. With all that yelling and anger, what else could you expect?

"Married people frequently ask me why I don't get married. I respond with 'why do you stay married when you're so miserable?' "

THREE

Alone Is Not Lonely

I never found the companion that was so companionable as solitude. We are for the most part more lonely when we go abroad among men than when we stay in our chambers. A man thinking or working is always alone, let him be where he will.
—HENRY DAVID THOREAU

I LIVE ALONE, and am frequently asked if I am lonely. I am puzzled by the assumption that the presence of another person in the house precludes loneliness. I am especially bemused when the question is posed by a couple who haven't spoken a civil word to each other in years except maybe "pass the salt."

A very wise and lovely elderly relative of mine was asked after her husband of fifty-years died whether she might not be lonely. She answered with a sad smile:

"Sometimes you can be lonelier living with someone than living alone."

According to *The American Heritage Dictionary of the English Language*, the definition of loneliness is "Dejected by the awareness of being alone." Thus it is a condition that is not a fact but merely a personal reaction to the situation of singleness. It's not the presence of people that prevents loneliness, it's the presence of a sense of self adequacy.

Being by yourself can be a liberation from those conscious or subconscious pulls that force you to cater to the needs of others. If your self-importance has been built on how well you respond to the demands of people around you, then you have never given yourself a chance to understand what really makes you happy. Being alone affords you the luxury of learning about YOU.

Widows who have spent a lifetime busily taking care of their families and have rarely spent a moment alone profess to be lonely at first until they learn the lovely self-indulgence of doing what they want and building their lives around their needs and not someone else's.

The Luxury of Being Alone

A divorced woman I know whose daughter went off to college reported that instead of the lonely empty nest depression everyone predicted, she experienced a soaring sense of glorious freedom.

"I don't have to listen to blasting rock music any more. I don't have to have my phone tied up for hours. I'm *free*."

Being alone can be a wonderful soul-nurturing state—if you enjoy your own company. There is tremendous pleasure in giving yourself the luxury of time to mull and muse about your feelings and reactions to the day's activities—in peaceful solitude. And to do just what you want without worrying about others' opinions.

A woman I interviewed who had a live-in relationship took a long distance phone call from him while we were talking.

"You'll be home tonight?" Her face fell. "I thought you were coming home next week. OK—see you." She hung up and said, "Nuts. I was so looking forward to a week alone." And went on to explain that living together was not always easy.

"It's just that he has an opinion on everything— and lets me know. Even when I schedule a manicure, he'll say 'Again? You just had one.' I love him, but I wish he'd keep out of my life a little."

There are evenings when you may want to burst

into the house and share the day's happenings with someone who cares like when you were a child and dashed home to tell your mother about the A in History. But there are those many evenings when you fall in exhausted and long to just unwind quietly. After you've cooled down, had your drink and dinner and feel like talking, that's when you get on the phone and chat with friends to your heart's content, without annoying interruptions demanding how much longer you intend to blab and snide allusions to the motor-mouth propensities of women.

Eating Alone & Loving It

One of the most frequent questions we live-alone's get from people who are curious about coping with singles living is the "Eating Alone" issue which I view as a Rorschach Test for positive vs. negative self-image.

"You don't cook for yourself, do you . . . just one person? I guess you eat a sandwich or something over the sink or get those frozen prepared things."

I tried one of those so-called gourmet microwave dinners once, and after the second bite which only confirmed the first, I thought the best thing about this meal was that I won't have to claim my luggage afterward.

Why not cook for myself . . . don't I count? Am I only worthy of a decent meal if I eat in consort?

Eating alone can be one of life's most satisfying epicurean experiences. Like all working people, I am tired at the end of the day. I find it extremely relaxing to set up a glass of wine on the kitchen counter, turn on the radio and begin the pleasant but mindless preparation of a fine meal. At this present moment, brown rice with onions, mushrooms, walnuts and sultanas is cooking on the stove and a cheese-and-zucchini casserole is in the oven while the scallops, garlic and parsley wait in the fridge for last-minute sautéeing. The table in the dining room is set with a place mat and bookstand and when my dinner is ready, I will take the phone off the hook, change the country western radio station I cook with to a classical music station which will assure me Bach or Mozart during dinner, set up my book and wine glass and sit down to savor the flavors of the food. This doesn't make me out to be an unsocialized misanthrope but just a person who luxuriates in the rewards of solitude as well as the conviviality of dining with company. I am happy with myself and, although I love dinner parties and dining with friends, I also enjoy eating alone without the cacophony of conversation that often serves to detract from rather than deepen the sensuous satisfaction that can be derived from fine fare.

I have heard many people say they can't bear eating alone. When I travel, which I do frequently to make TV and radio appearances and present seminars, I usually eat in hotel dining rooms. It used to be a common sight to see men at tables for one; now there are just as many women dining in solitary splendor. A friend of mine was horrified to hear that I can do this.

"If I were alone in a hotel, I'd never go down to the dining room. I'd have them send up room service."

A good part of her reaction, along with those who will not dine alone, comes not from fear of aloneness but rather of reluctance to be publicly viewed as unwanted, the old double-standard whereby he is alone by choice and she by rejection. That, of course, is nonsense. As is the old bromide that a lone woman is scorned by the maître d' and relegated automatically to a seat next to the kitchen. I have been traveling alone and eating alone for years, and the only time I ever ran into a male/female situation was in a Harley hotel dining room in Columbus, Ohio. I waited behind a single man who was asked by the hostess if he wished to be seated at the "travelers' table," which was a large banquet-looking setup filled with men, "and you get a free drink on the house, too" she added with a smile. When my turn came, she said, "One?" and started to lead me to a table. "Wait a moment," I said, "Don't I get offered the free drink and the 'travelers' table'?" "Oh no," she answered immediately, "That's for men only." I looked at her and said evenly, "Really? That's illegal. Sex discrimination is against the law." She became upset and her face turned beet red. It had apparently never dawned on her or the management that a policy innovated to make life pleasanter for the traveling man could also apply to the traveling woman. She apologized and after I assured her I had no wish to be

seated with a bunch of strangers, but would not refuse a free drink, she put me at a lovely quiet ban-
quette and brought me a bloody mary and a bottle of
wine on the house.

There are many people who shrink at the idea of
being alone or doing things alone simply because
they have never tried it and fear they will suffer from
that nebulous undefined condition of "loneliness."
It's not scary to be by yourself, it's wonderful. Loneliness is not a state of being, it's just a state of mind.

FOUR

No Way Wedlock

For what is wedlock forced, but a hell,
An age of discord and continual
    strife?
Whereas the contrary bringest bliss
And is a pattern of celestial peace.
—WILLIAM SHAKESPEARE, *King Henry VI*

DEBBIE REYNOLDS tried to get Frank Sinatra to marry her and move to Scarsdale in a movie called *The Tender Trap*. Doris Day was forever virginally unapproachable until Rock Hudson agreed to matrimony. Marriage was the goal of the leading ladies in hundreds of movies of the 1940's and fifties and it was a universal assumption that connubial bliss was craved by females and dodged by men and the inevitable

67

ending to every made-in-Hollywood courtship was that she snared him and they lived happily ever after.

Times have changed. Hollywood has changed. They no longer make "movies," mere frivolous forms of mass entertainment; we now get "films" designed to contribute to their concept of the human condition, God help us. Current films and TV depict women who dump men because they need "space." In fact, that word is being used as a dramatic device so frequently that it gives new meaning to the term "space age." Women are as likely to be the deserters as the desertees and cohabitation rather than commitment is often *her* choice. The hit TV series "Family Ties" has Alex pining for love of his girlfriend who opted to go off to Paris rather than continue their relationship. And the plots of "Duet," another popular series, revolve around Laura's resistance to Ben's plaintive pleas for marriage.

No Longer Longing to Marry

Does art mirror life or does life mirror art? In a free society such as ours, it happens in a simultaneous explosion. Judging from what we see and hear both in the real world and the world of make-believe, we must accept as an inescapable fact that today not all women long to marry. And for a variety of reasons, many women actively avoid matrimony and regard the lifestyle as antithetical to happiness.

Marriage can be a very happy way of life and

there are millions of couples who enjoy the relationship and millions more entering into it. But we now recognize that there are alternatives that are equally acceptable. Marriage is no longer regarded as the only way to live, but merely as one of the possible lifestyles one may choose to adopt.

If you want further proof of societal recognition and respect for the woman's right to remain single, witness the total acceptance of the term "Ms." that eliminated the former stigmatization of the spinster brought about by making a "Miss" identify herself as different and somewhat lesser than a "Mrs."

Marriage creates male/female role assignments that can destroy relationships rather than cement them. Women who feel that they cannot or will not conform to the confines of this dictum may now opt to skip the whole construct and live with a man and derive all the pleasures of conjugality with none of the restrictions.

* * *

Joanne and Jeff had been living together for five years and are solidly set into a happy, loving joint existence that combines the conventional components of connubial togetherness with the romantic aura of courtship.

The house they had just bought showed signs of the extensive do-it-yourself renovation that they were doing together. There was a casual, inviting warmth to the decor and Joanne projected the secure contentment of a women who knew what she wanted and was fortunate enough to have it. The scene was perfect. The only items missing were the picket fence—and the marriage license.

"Jeff would get married tomorrow. But not me. Marriage is just a piece of paper that could have a negative impact. This relationship is the best thing that's ever happened to me and no way am I going to rock the boat. Everything is wonderful as is—why do something that might change it?"

Joanne is an attractive, vivacious thirty-eight-year-old woman who had been married at nineteen and divorced at twenty-one. "It wasn't anyone's fault. When I got married, I expected to live happily ever after. Like magic. After a while, I realized something was very wrong only I didn't know what. I had this crazy, unreal image of a wife and a husband and I was angry and upset all the time because neither of us could fill our roles. He couldn't manage what I thought men were supposed to handle in a marriage, and I didn't want to be the kind of person I thought a wife had to be. It was really dumb. But all I could see was me becoming one of those women like my mother who can't drive and I went nuts."

Hers was the classic case of a marriage that failed because of the commonest of reasons, unrealistic expectations. Joanne is naturally aggressive and independent but she believed that implicit in "I do" was that she *not* do and that overnight the marriage ceremony would change her into a submissive Suzy homemaker and her husband into a strong take-charge guy. When she realized she detested being a helpless female and resented that her new husband (who was all of twenty) didn't instantly know how to balance a checkbook and handle family finances, she felt trapped and furious. It was untenable and they divorced.

Thenceforth Joanne regarded marriage as the worst form of bondage. She saw it as a destructive force that changed lives and altered psyches and personalities. In a sense, she was right. The old adage that you don't know someone until you live with him or her is true, except that often the someone you don't know is YOU. There is no way you can anticipate how you will react to living with another person until you do it. There is give and take in every relationship but how do you know how much you can give or take until you are there? It is easy to assume you know yourself and your levels of tolerance toward specific behaviors. But what you cannot predict is your willingness to lower those threshholds of acceptance in response to signs of love and kindness that bring you joy and happiness. You cannot stand boorishness and it drives you nuts when your guy tells tasteless jokes that indicate to you an important lack of sophistication and sensitivity. You grind your teeth and swear that the next time he does it, you're out of there. But on your birthday he surprised you by bringing a cake to your office and when you were sick he insisted on staying home from work in order to take care of you. How can you not love living with a guy like that? It's a tradeoff . . . like everything else in life.

Marriage Can Create
Unrealistic Expectations

"I love our life together," continued Joanne. "I can't see where marriage could add anything positive but I have seen where it could be a big negative. Getting married almost destroyed my friend's relationship. She had been living with her friend for eight years. They were great together until they decided they wanted kids, so they got married.

"The minute they became husband and wife, everything went haywire. She expected some kind of magic transformation . . . like he would suddenly act like a Husband, whatever that meant. For instance, she was furious because he couldn't rewire the kitchen. A husband is supposed to do handyman things, right? That's what her Dad did, so of course all husbands should. For gosh sakes, the guy had trouble screwing in a light bulb and now she expects him to be Mr. Goodwrench? Here they had been going along happy as clams, enjoying life and then this big ceremony takes place and everything changes because she figures they have to get serious now and make a Life Plan, set up a budget, buckle down to the business of living and she becomes a major nag.

"They nearly broke up but a little therapy helped straighten things out and they made it OK. But who needs that? Jeff and I are happy just the way we are and to my mind there's absolutely no benefit in going through some legal stuff. What for? I've seen it too many times, when they get the piece of paper expectations change and suddenly everything's supposed to be perfect. Things they used to do or not do, or used to let slide, are not acceptable any more. Jeff and I, we just take life as it comes and we're happy."

Joanne had met Jeff in her office. She was a manager with the telephone company where he works as a technician.

"He's shy," she said with a laugh. "I had to ask him out. Twice! We dated and then it began to develop into something good. After a year, it had passed the infatuation stage and grown into love. Then I lost the lease on my apartment and had to find a place to live. It just seemed natural for me to move in with Jeff."

Buying the house was also a practical decision. At income tax time, their accountant pointed out how much money they were sending down the tax tubes by not having the benefits of deductibles like mortgage interest. They had minor difficulty in getting a joint mortgage since they were not married. "The bank asked us for a 'statement of relationship' which I thought was nonsense. If we bought the property together as an investment, no one would question it. But since we intended to live there, that somehow changed things. We put ourselves down as 'spousal equivalents,' " she said with a big laugh "and they accepted it." Now they delight in owning their own home and at the slow casual pace that suits them both, are renovating the place a bit at a time. The house has three bedrooms—their room, a den, and a guest room. No nursery, and none anticipated.

"We don't want children," she said emphatically. "We decided that early on and haven't changed our minds. In fact, we're so definite that this year Jeff had a vasectomy."

For two years after her divorce, Joanne had worked in a facility for abused and neglected children. She spent her days with children of all ages and often had the satisfaction of helping to turn around the life of an almost doomed child.

Although she likes children, she realized that she does not have the patience for the responsibility of a day-to-day relationship and does not have the desire or talent for parenting.

"I have twenty-one nieces and nephews and I dearly love them all. We have great times together, they know I'm for fun and their mothers are for serious. I really enjoy spending the day with one or two at a time, and I can be patient and totally free with them because I know that in a couple of hours I can go home to peace and quiet and relax. I make a marvelous aunt, but I'd make a lousy mother."

Joanne grew up in an Irish-Catholic family of ten children. "If you haven't shared a four-bedroom one-bathroom house with twelve people, you can't understand the pleasures of privacy and the joys of living with just one person.

"My parents had some marriage. We never heard raised voices in our house because they never spoke to each other, except about household and family things. My father worked two jobs, so he wasn't around all that much and when he was home, he was tired. I never heard them exchange a word about their feelings, I never saw them kiss each other. Their only relationship was in producing ten babies. We have friends today with that kind of marriage; if it

weren't for their kids there wouldn't be anything between them at all."

Parental Pressure
to Marry

Coming from a strongly religious home as she
did, Joanne anticipated some remonstration and
shock from her parents when she and Jeff moved in
together.

"I was the first of my friends to divorce. You
have to know that in our house the word 'divorce'
was like the 'F' curseword. So I figured my mom and
dad would be horrified because I was 'living in sin.'
But not at all. They see how happy Jeff and I are and
how we live a quiet life. We don't have wild parties or
hang out in bars. My father's only comment was, 'I
guess it's OK as long as you're happy.' And my
mother's reaction when I told her I did not intend to
marry or have children, was simply, 'If that's how
God meant for you to be, then it's right.' That was the
closest I've felt to my mother in my whole life and I'm
grateful we had that chance to finally touch each
other. She died last year."

The Freedom
of Non-Marriage

Although Joanne and Jeff display a commitment
to a shared future, there is an undercurrent of inde-

pendence in her demeanor that adds to rather than subtracts from her obvious sense of security. She has learned that being alone is taking responsibility for oneself as everyone must ultimately do in order to survive. Trust and interdependability are integral parts of any good relationship, but dependence leads to subordination and the eventual diminishing of self.

"I admit I like keeping my eye on the exit door. And I like not having to be beholden to anyone. Like when I got this great job offer that meant leaving the telephone company where Jeff and I work. Now no one leaves the telephone company, a job there is for life. But this sounded so exciting and such a terrific opportunity, and besides, I like the stimulation of change. I wanted to talk it over with Jeff, but he was away on a hunting trip that week. So I made the decision myself and took the job and I love it. If we were married, I'd *have* to discuss it with my husband. Not being married makes me feel that I have more control over my own life. And that's what I must have."

The Restrictions of Marriage

"Love is consideration, and marriage is obligation. When that certificate comes, the whole feeling changes."

This came from twenty-five-year-old Melissa who has lived with the man she loves for over two years and has finally gotten him to understand that her refusal to marry is not a rejection of him but an important affirmation of self for her.

Melissa comes from a small town in the midwest and came east to college. She met Paul through friends and they fell in love quickly. But her schedule and his job resulted in their seeing each other on weekends only, "We had dates, like Bobby and Margie going to the maltshop." After they talked and talked and learned about each other's background, childhood, feelings about life and issues, and sated the tremendous hunger to know all about the one you love from the moment of birth, they realized they wanted more than just the dating relationship.

"I heard him telling our friends about occurrences of the day that I hadn't heard before. And we knew we wanted to live together, to see each other at breakfast, and to know we would see each other every night. So I moved into his apartment."

Their parents were puzzled. If you love each other, why not marry? But Melissa had associations with the word marriage that she knew would destroy their relationship. So they have been living together happily, and intend to do so indefinitely.

"Marriage would change me, I know it," she says. "I can't bear the thought of being cast into a mold. I would feel restricted, typecast and I'd hate it. Right now, I do all the 'female' things in the house— the cooking, shopping and cleaning. I do it because if I didn't, the place would be a pigsty and we'd eat fast food every night. Paul is a slob and he just doesn't care. But if we married, somehow I would resent being pushed into that role because it's expected, demanded. To me it would be a tyranny I couldn't endure."

Melissa has worked hard on herself to become self-sufficient and independent and she sees marriage as a threat to all she has accomplished. "I love Paul, and right now I want to spend the rest of my life with him. But I know that I'm a better person because we're not married. I wouldn't like me, he wouldn't like me and it would all end up in disaster."

Melissa is burdened with the image of her mother, and grandmother, and all the women she knew who lived conventional homemaker lives and never questioned their roles. Women were the ones who had the responsibility of making the marriage work, with little input or emotional support from their husbands. She had a father who was never "there for us" and a mother who accepted the deprivation as women historically have done. She saw the marital male hierarchy of the dominant father and the subordinate wife, and the injustices imposed and feared that being married would make her view herself as one of those pathetic subservient wretches and would destroy her love for Paul and his for her.

"I meet women who think marriage gives them stability and reliability. I see it as doing just the opposite to me. It would make me shaky because I would lose confidence in myself and my own ability to make decisions."

Like so many young women who have grown up through the women's movement, Melissa is keenly aware of the difficulty women go through in order to be accepted at parity by men. A great part of the travail is the personal struggle to build belief in your own strength and power before you can expect to be viewed as equal. She had fought that battle and saw marriage as a threat to her hard-won strength and self-sufficiency.

"Right now, Paul wants us to do everything as a couple. He has a much greater need than I to be together. I want us to have three lives—his, mine, and ours—but he wants one only. When I'm stuck at work, I call and he gives me a hard time because he hates when I'm late. I love him and don't like to make him unhappy, but if I was married I would feel more obligated to be home on time. Now I feel freer to do what is right for me. If I got a wonderful job offer in another part of the country, or wanted to relocate to a different climate, we would talk it over. I can't see ever wanting to leave Paul because I love him so much. But if he just balked arbitrarily and I felt strongly that I had to go, I would feel free to do so. I couldn't do that if we were married. I can't envision that happening, but I need to know that I could. I'm here with Paul because I want to be, not because I have to be."

You Can't Rite the Wrongs

"Lots of our friends got married and divorced—even before they paid off their VISA card expenses for the wedding. I don't know what miracle they expected to happen when they got married, but obviously it didn't."

Relationships are built on love and trust, not ritual. Many of Melissa's friends thought that marriage would cement relationships and convert what were merely preliminary facades into permanent installations. It doesn't work that way. If there isn't enough there to hold things together before marriage, going through a rite will not correct the wrong. Instead of giving their feelings for each other a chance to develop, they regarded marriage as an acceleration device: "Once we're husband and wife, we'll have the sense of commitment to make it work." Then they go through all the months of festive build-up planning for the wedding, consuming brides' magazines, buying the gown, selecting bridesmaids, silver patterns, invitations and get carried away with the magic moment concept that says they will get married and live happily ever after.

Finally the big event takes place. All the frenzied months of planning are consummated, it's all over and suddenly they are no longer basking in the golden glow of being the special fussed-over bride-and-groom center of attention ("What a beautiful bride she made!" "Wasn't it a gorgeous wedding?"). Now they are alone together, nothing special, just another married couple . . . and then comes the letdown. To their shock, the experience, no matter how costly, enchanting and glorious, hasn't changed either one an iota. If there were things about each other that bothered them before, being married did not erase them. Marriage is not a rite of purification. In fact, if anything, you are even more annoyed because you are now dealing with disappointment over your unrealistic expectation that the ceremony would be a cure-all. You're angry because things did not become perfect instantly and being married did not make either of you different people than you were before. So marriage becomes the problem, not the solution.

"It's Easier to NOT Get Married"

Rose, a vivavious woman who just turned thirty-nine, and Joe, a handsome, athletic-looking man of forty-four, have been living together for more than ten years and she never once entertained the idea of getting married.

"What for?" says Rose. "Getting married is an active step . . . it involves going out and doing something for what seems to me to be no real reason at all. We're together, we're a team, we love each other, what will the piece of paper do for us that we don't already have?"

Rose works in the computer industry as does Joe. Recently, they decided to join forces and started a business together. "So we already have a legal tie—we're incorporated," said Rose.

Ten years ago, they started out with a purely sexual relationship that grew into something much more. Each had lived through many lifestyle changes, and this seemed to be, at first, merely another casual encounter. They soon perceived that they wanted to be with each other all the time, and finally moved in together. Over the years, they had their fights, ups and downs, and identity crises.

"I'm much more confident now then I used to be," says Rose. "More demanding, because I have a pride in myself that took years to build. And Joe helped but it's made his life with me a little tougher. He sometimes feels somewhat threatened but he wants us to stay together so he's changed, too. If you were to ask who gives more, who compromises more I'd say that for the first five years, I gave 70 percent and he 30 percent. During the last five years, the figures have flipped. But I've never said I'd leave because the one good thing I got from my mother was that you have to stick with it."

Like most women, Rose's reaction to marriage was colored by her perception of her parents' relationship. Her mother was an immigrant who married an American southerner whose business took him away from home a great deal. An only child, she and her mother were alone much of the time and her mother's resentment and sense of abandonment were a constant source of discussion. Rose grew up with a jaundiced view of the institution of marriage, and for years could not understand her mother's prodding Rose to get married when she herself was so obviously unhappy with the results.

"The whole thought of marriage is scary," says Rose. "I do not want to live like my mother and father did. There's an eternity aspect to the whole thing that I don't like. Sure, I'd like to have someone next to me in twenty years, but marriage doesn't guarantee that."

Neither Joe nor Rose want children. They feel that there are plenty of people out there reproducing and keeping mankind going. If they want to make an impact on the next generation, there are lots of ways to work with children to pass along their knowledge.

In every aspect of their life, they live like a married couple. Joe cooks because he's better at it. They worry about each other and feel responsible to each other. In fact, during the interview I had with Rose, she looked at her watch constantly and then excused herself to call Joe to say she would be late and he should have dinner without her. When I pointed this out to her, she said: "Of course we're considerate of each other because we care for each other. That's love, not necessarily marriage. Marriage is purely a social tradition that has no impact on the reality of living with someone. It's supposed to give permanence, but I assure you that if either one of us was unhappy and wanted out, that piece of paper wouldn't hold us."

Flexibility, Freedom & Romance, Too

There is an aura to unwedded bliss that was apparent in each woman I interviewed, a sense of certainty about themselves, a pride and happiness that comes from feeling loved, secure and excited with life. Although none of them voiced it, they are subconsciously proud of themselves for breaking the rules and winning.

Granted that it's easier today than ever before to live together without benefit of clergy, you are still fighting the battle of convention and parental pressure. The way society is set up, it is passive to get married and active to avoid it. Yet these women have had the courage to decide what is right for them regardless of tradition and the behavior of others. None of them is a radical, or in any way different in appearance or action than their peers. They are just ordinary folks, but remember it's just "ordinary folks" who have historically proven to be the catalysts of change. Like the little boy in "The Emperor's Clothes" who was unafraid to point out that the emperor was naked, these women have pointed out that marriage ain't what it's been cracked up to be and should no longer be regarded as a given.

Another important quality that was palpably obvious in every home I visited that is not always present in married households was Romance. Besides the love, caring and other elements that also exist in successful marriages, there is the romantic excitement generated from his and her knowledge that she is there with him only because she wants to be and not because of the bonds of law or children or convention . . . that she is free and flexible and as ready as men have always been to take off should he fail her or the relationship become unfulfilling.

Erich Segal said in his best-selling novel *Love Story* that love means never having to say you're sorry. Cynthia Smith says that living together without marriage means you never have to worry about being taken for granted.

FIVE

The Motherhood Option: Non-Mothers and Single Mothers

The choice of a point of view is the initial act
of a culture.
>   —JOSE ORTEGA Y GASSET

MOTHERHOOD, the flag and apple pie had always
been regarded as the sacred American trilogy . . . re-
vered and unassailable. The Vietnam War protestors
showed us that the flag could be savaged and the

85

country would survive. Custard and quiche probably outpull apple in overall national pie consumption. And today, women can announce that they do not want children and not be stoned in public. We live in an era where everyone comes out of the closet and admits very personal heretofore private feelings and proclivities without risk of ostracization.

A couple of my friends opted thirty years ago to not have children. One is an attorney and the other a merchandising executive. But they are such high-powered women that no one dared to question their choice. However, I can remember two aunts who were pitied as failed wives because they had no children. And other women who chose to forego motherhood and were disbelieved as people whispered behind their backs: "So I wonder whose fault it is—his or hers?"

The Death of Momism

Now it's out in the open. Not all women want to be mothers. Not all of them believe that a woman's only route toward the fulfillment of her destiny is to bring up children. Although the maternal urge has always been regarded as a universal female trait, we are now finding out that it is not. And here in the iconoclastic eighties, another dogma bites the dust, the nomism of momism is dead. According to Shere Hite's *Women in Love*, "Not all women want to have children; recent figures have shown that twice as many couples as ten years ago have decided not to have children."

So why do we still make women who do not have children defend their position? Why do we use the word "childless" which implies that to have a child is the natural state and to be without offspring is to be in some way less? Because as usual, society has not yet caught up with contemporary changes in behavior—but we're getting there.

All of the women described in the previous chapters (with the exception of Melissa) stated emphatically that they did not want children, as did many other women I interviewed.

Marriage No Longer the Means to Motherhood

For those women who do want children, marriage as the necessary means to motherhood has also lost its luster as a lodestar. Again citing Shere Hite, "Wanting to have children is not always connected in women's minds with getting married: women can have children alone now, after all, and many women who are married when they have a child find that they wind up raising the child alone anyway. Aside from frequent financial difficulties, many women and children do not find that this is an unhappy way of life at all. The number of single, never-married women with children is 2 percent of the United States female population: U.S. Census figures show that in 1985 there were 7.7 million female single heads of households with children between one and seventeen years of age."

In a report called "Americans' Marital Status and Living Arrangements" issued by the Census Bureau and prepared by Arlene F. Saluter of the Marriage and Family Statistics Branch, it was estimated that 24 percent of U.S. children live with just one parent. 14.8 million youngsters under the age of 18 were living with one parent in 1986, up from 5.8 million in 1960. Of the children living in one-parent households, 27 percent were children of parents who had never married.

* * *

Erin, a beautiful willowy thirty-seven-year-old woman, decided that she wanted to have a child before she was thirty so at age twenty-eight she bore a son.

"I was not in a relationship at the time, nor did any of the past men I'd known strike me as the kind of person I wanted to marry and spend my life with, so I had my baby with the boyfriend I was seeing then. He knew I wanted to be pregnant and he told me that as far as he was concerned it was strictly my affair—and that was fine with me."

Today, her eight-year-old son is a great source of pleasure to her and she is totally happy with her decision to be a single mother. "I was a child of the wild sixties, when everything was going on and the women's movement was taking hold. The idea of marriage never entered my mind."

In that era, no one thought too much of the future and the need for forever commitment to one person was not high on their agenda. As Erin moved into her thirties, she had some long-term relationships, but they never seemed to be the right ones.

"I like being on my own. I'm comfortably happy, why should I be with someone who makes me and my son even slightly unhappy? It's a whole lot better being lonely by yourself then lonely with someone who gives you a false idea of companionship and makes you feel trapped.

"I like the energy between man and woman, and I sometimes think I would like to fall in love. But these days I'm in control, and I find that falling in love is based on your desire to fall in love. So maybe I don't really want what could be a disturbing element. I'm very contented with my son and my life, and I can't see where marriage offers me anything, except maybe financial help that I could always use. But it's such a risk—I would hate to face the hassle of getting out of it if it's wrong."

Erin has recently gone back to college and discovered she has a flair for computers which can lead to a lucrative career. Since she is totally self-supporting and money is frequently a problem, she is very excited about her future.

"My son is in school all day and so am I. It's great."

He is a poised, happy child who is active and happy. Erin attributes this to the stability of his home life as contrasted with so many of his friends who have divorced parents. She points out that these children suffer through the bickering and bitterness that is usually concomitant with divorce, and whereas they are never sure where they will be when and with whom, her son always knows his home and mother are a dependable certainty.

"I'm independent. I like my life just as it is—I wouldn't want to change a thing," she said with a very contented smile.

As more and more women enter their thirties still not having found the man they wish to spend their lives with, the option to have a child without marriage is becoming more attractive and almost commonplace. If she is financially secure, has her own apartment or house and wants to share her life with a child but not a man, why not become a single mother?

Single Parent Status

In an article about women lawyers in the March 8, 1988 issue of *The New York Times Magazine*, one of the success stories depicted Peggy L. Kerr, who in 1981 became the first woman partner of Skadden, Arps, Slate, Meagher & Flom, one of the nation's largest law firms employing more than eight hundred attorneys.

"Peggy Kerr, for example, has never married, a

circumstance she says is linked to the demands of her career. In 1983, unwilling to forgo the experience of motherhood, she adopted an infant daughter, Amalia, and recently she adopted a son, Brian, now six months old. . . . 'Family was extremely important to me,' Peggy Kerr says of her decision to become a single parent. . . . She worried how Skadden's partners would react to her single-motherhood. Her female colleagues were immediately supportive. As it turns out, her male colleagues did not appear to be fazed by her single-parent status. They lined up outside her office to hold Amalia when Kerr returned from a three-month maternity leave. 'Amalia had eighty-five uncles,' Kerr jokes."

When single parenthood is accepted with such *sang froid* by that most conservative of enclaves, the big city law firm, and is reported openly in the non-sensational media, then you know that the stigma is gone. Further proof of the current acceptability of single parenthood was the February 1988 newspaper account of the prevalence of unwed maternity in that bastion of convention, the U.S. Navy. A study by Commander Judy J. Glenn, a nurse in the obstetrics and gynecology department of the San Diego Naval Hospital, found that nearly 41 percent of the enlisted women who became pregnant in a recent ten-month period were single.

More and more luminaries are having babies out of wedlock. The expression "born on the other side of the blanket" is virtually unknown today while the word bastard is used for cursing rather than describing illegitimacy, another archaic term. Mia Farrow and Woody Allen are pictured in the media as proud parents of their newly born son; Farah Fawcett and Ryan O'Neal have children and neither couple had indicated any desire or need to marry. The outraged denunciation that was heaped on Ingrid Bergman years ago when she dared to have twins with Roberto Rosselini without benefit of marriage seems laughable today. If the moral climate has changed so radically within only twenty years, then think how totally acceptable and commonplace children of unmarried mothers will be when they grow up in the next twenty years? According to a cover story in *Newsweek* in 1986, "The Single Parent," by 1990 half of all households may well be headed by single parents, mostly women.

The Passing of the "Normal Home"

When I was a child, I cannot recall one friend whose parents were divorced. And I had a lot of friends. How many children can say that today? With the current divorce rate hovering around 50 percent, single parent households are as conventional as mom-and-dad homes. Children tend to dislike being unlike their peers and where years ago a child of divorce would have suffered from feeling painfully different, today in some neighborhoods the kids of nuclear families are the rare birds. It's become like Hollywood where criss-crossing of parents was always prevalent. Remember the old joke of two movie stars' children fighting when one threatens the other "I'll get my father to beat up your father!" and the other one answers "But my father *is* your father!"

Marriage and motherhood are no longer the necessary combination. Melissa, who was interviewed in a previous chapter and lives with a man whom she has no intention of marrying, stated that she wants children when she reaches her mid-thirties, and intends to have them.

"What's the difference to our kids if we are married? We're just 'Mom and Dad,' just like my parents were. Why would it even enter their minds to ask? Do you remember ever asking your parents if they were married? Besides, by that time it will be so common that marriage will not even be an issue."

If you have any concern that children brought up with only mothers will be in any way warped, research studies conducted for *The Hite Report* on men indicated that such children do well in both careers and personal relationships. In fact, boys who spend most of their childhoods with only their mothers have better relationships with women later, are more verbal and less competitive in relationships than boys who grow up with both parents.

The decision to have a baby without a live-in father is not one to be taken lightly. Having another parent to share the problems and pleasures that arise in the raising of a child is indeed wonderful and there will be moments when you may feel deprived and torn and wonder whether you have been fair in depriving your child of a so-called normal home. The consolations here may come by realizing that there is no longer such a thing as a "normal home" since normalcy is determined by numbers and single parent homes may be on a par with two-parent families. Although at the time of crisis one longs to have another person who shares your concerns to help make critical decisions, it is good to remember that split thinking could be a drawback rather than a boon, and that the need to argue with a father over what you and he think is right could be aggravating as well as destructive. Another factor to be considered in your decision process is the complaint so many married woman make about their husbands' lack of involvement in bringing up their children, that many of them find that they are, in effect "single mothers." The bodily presence of another parent doesn't necessarily mean shared responsibility. Single mothers usually develop a network of relatives and friends who supply the warm family background in which to nurture the growth and development of a child.

Single motherhood may or may not be the route you select, but it is good to know that it is a viable option for your future.

SIX

They Wanted to Marry in the Worst Way . . . and They Did

Keep your eyes wide open before marriage,
half shut afterwards.
> —BENJAMIN FRANKLIN,
> *Poor Richard's Almanac*

SHE HAS REACHED THE PINNACLE, the fulfillment of the female America dream . . . she's *married!* She is permitted to be smug and satisfied because she is now regarded as a valuable Woman and, at least in her mother's eyes, more successful than her friend who is a vice-president of Morgan Stanley but still piteously single. She should be happy. So why isn't she?

We marry for a myriad of reasons but mostly because it is expected of us and we have been instructed that the family unit is the basis of our society and only by conforming to that construct will we be accepted, fulfilled and consequently happy. We are also given to understand that, like any convention, those who do not follow the rules will be "Outsiders," forever forced to deal with questions. But isn't it preferable to endure the annoyance of raised eyebrows rather than the pain of unfulfilled dreams? The raised eyebrows are on passing faces whose concerns for you are casual, and to trade in your hopes in order to say "yes" to the careless questions "Are you married?" is foolish to the point of tragic.

The Doctor's Wife

Marcia was a bright, awkward and untidy girl who was class president in high school, liked by girls and admired but never adored by boys. She grew up in a community that was renowned for its affluence but was actually a mix of modest to millionaire homes where socializing was based on interest rather than income and class distinctions were blurred. Marcia's academician parents' unconcern for esthetics and luxuries were obvious from the slapdash look of their home which was furnished in early Salvation Army. Her mother was an extremely unattractive woman who seemed to feel that having snared a handsome achieving husband relieved her of the necessity of even attempting to look appealing. Like many children who are brought up in a household where money and its attendant pleasures are unimportant, Marcia and her younger brother craved riches. "I'm going to be a doctor and make lots of money," she announced, and applied to the top level colleges which would route her to medical school acceptance. It did not go easily for Marcia, nothing did, and she was turned down by all-but-one good school where last minute wait listing paid off and she was accepted.

She worked hard because she knew that high marks were mandatory if one sought admission to crowded U.S. medical schools. College was demanding but she was determined—and lonely. Then she met Glenn in one of her classes and for the first time found a man who thought her attractive. She fell madly in love. What she did not know was that Glenn found all women attractive and had a lusty sex drive that took him from one bed to the other with promiscuous regularity. She saw him whenever he wished and slept with him at will—his. Totally infatuated and virtually enslaved, her schoolwork suffered and for the first time her grades slipped below the A's and B's required for med school admission. Then came the worst blow of all. She got herpes, an incurable venereal infection which she knew had to have come from Glenn since he was the first and only man with whom she had sex. She confronted him with her anger and he deflected it casually by seducing her again. The destructive relationship persisted all through college although she tried to break it up from time to time but like all obsessed victims of unrequited passions, could never resist Glenn's demands.

By the time she was graduated, Marcia had managed to pull up her point average but, demoralized by Glenn's behavior, her M-CAT medical school qualifying exam performance was lacklustre. She knew she could do far better and decided to take the exam again the next year when she felt that a stronger M-CAT score further enhanced by working laboratory experience could improve her candidacy. To that end, she took a job as a biologist in a hospital. There she met the second man in her life, Richard, a medical student.

Like her father, Richard was handsome and taciturn. Marcia was intelligent and sociable and enjoyed stimulating conversation but recognized that men did not have the same talent as women for chitchat and small talk. Richard was unable to show affection other than sexually but seemed to have an attachment to her that she found gratifying. However, his long silences and unwillingness or inability to engage in any kind of discussion or interchange of ideas bothered her. She never mentioned her concerns to him because how could plain undeserving Marcia dare to make demands upon a handsome male for whose attentions she should be grateful? However, she did complain about his sullenness to her mother whose reaction was predictable.

"So what if he doesn't talk much. He's a *doctor*. And he's so *handsome*. What more could any girl want? Men are like that. You want conversation, call me!"

Like all medical students, Richard was work driven and exhausted a good deal of the time. In order to see each other, it seemed more convenient to have Marcia move into his apartment where she could take care of the household needs easier than he since she just had a nine-to-five job. Their life became a routine of see-you-sometimes, supper and sex as his schedule allowed. As the year went on, the required care and feeding of Richard plus her job made it more difficult for Marcia to find time to study for the retaking of her M-CATs. The continued pressure from her mother didn't help.

"Why bother with med school—it will be three years out of your life and even if you do get in, how do you know that Richard will wait? What about children? You want to have a family before you're too old. Marry him, and he'll be the doctor in the family."

Marcia longed to be a physician, to have the status, self-satisfaction, sense of personal achievement and security that the M.D. degree symbolized to her. She was not deeply in love with Richard but their sex life was good and they had developed an easy compatibility that was pleasant. If she passed this up, how did she know she would ever find another man who might want to marry her? And isn't being married and a mother the real measure of a woman's success? Unequipped with an ego to counter her mother's barrage of corrosive propaganda, Marcia began to believe that marriage to Richard would be the sensible fulfillment of any girl's dream. When her younger brother called with great excitement to say that he had just been accepted by the medical school she had her heart set on, Marcia felt her destiny was confirmed and she and Richard were married.

Three years later Marcia had a baby. Anyone who ran into her mother was treated to an unfurled six-pack of baby pictures accompanied by her triumphant trumpeting that her son was a doctor and her daughter a doctor's wife. She was totally fulfilled. But what about Marcia?

Marriage works well between two people who love and like each other and do not mind the overlooking of irksome differences required of a successful relationship. When either element is missing, however, the going is rocky. In the column "Hers," published in *The New York Times*, Patricia Volk wrote: "There isn't a woman I know who hasn't dreamed of killing her husband. . . . The person you live with . . . have babies with . . . is often the person you like least in the world." Marcia did not like Richard. He was a withholding person who could sit for hours at a dinnertable of chattering people and not utter a word. She rarely knew what he was thinking and began to care less. Furthermore, he was a doctor which automatically creates problems in the marriage department.

In my book *Doctors' Wives: The Truth About Medical Marriages* I pointed out that men who are doctors are usually obsessive compulsive individuals who, in order to attain the grades required for medical school admission, single mindedly drive themselves scholastically and thereby sacrifice the normal development of interpersonal skills along the way making them inept and immature in social situations. Since the donning of the magic white coats instantly endows them with godlike qualifications in the eyes of patients and patients' families, they never have the need to develop the socializer facet of their personalities. All too often they become arrogant and inflexible in all relationships. We learn how to act from signs of approval and disapproval elicited from others and tend to adjust our behavior to get the most possible positive reaction we can. After all, most of us want to be liked. But doctors say what they damned please and in any way they please because who's going to call them jerks? We are fearful of offending the great man who controls our survival, and would never dare to complain about his insensitivity, or crassness or frequently tactless cruelty. In normal social interaction, a person who speaks crudely or hurtfully is usually made aware of his gaffe immediately and if he has any sense and wants to be invited again, he cleans up his act at once and learns from the experience. But who's going to teach niceness to a doctor? No matter what he says and how he says it, everyone treats him with respect so he goes through life believing that he's a perfect charmer.

Richard fit the above profile in every detail and Marcia was miserable. But the insecurity that had dogged her all her life prevented her from admitting that she might be anything less than happy. After all, hadn't she achieved all the elements of successful womanhood . . . a husband, house and baby? She even had the money to live in the luxurious style she had longed for as a youngster. Her self-deception went on until she had a reunion with two friends she had not seen since for two years after she and Richard had moved away to another state where he found a practice that suited his needs.

The two young women were happy to see her and hear all about her life. One was an investment banker and the other an engineer and both exuded the confidence and pride of women who had achieved their goals and were contented with themselves. They had comfortable apartments, dressed well and travelled frequently both on vacations and business and had active social lives. The implicit assumption about reunions is that the only people who attend are those who are successful and/or gorgeous. Nobody goes to flaunt failure, which is why everyone returns from those affairs with the inevitable comment about how wonderful everyone looks. Of course, losers never come; only the winners show up. Marcia fully expected to be regarded as the winner of the three. After all, she alone had achieved all the accouterments of female success, marriage (to a doctor, yet) a baby and a house. What more could any woman want? To her disquiet, they oohed and aahed over the pictures of her baby and house without displaying any signs of envy and then went on to tell her about their lives, the creation and completion of important business deals, decisions that affected millions of people and dollars, involvement in research and development of advanced technological break-throughs. She found herself countering with tales of Richard's accomplishments.

Marcia felt dispirited that night and barely spoke to her husband, but he never noticed. She was now thirty-five, living with a man who gave her merely the bare bones of a pleasurable existence. But whose fault was that? She looked at him and realized that the person in the room she liked least at that moment was herself.

Marcia had accepted the mores of her mother and women of past generations even though she had choices that they did not. Her own insecurity and lack of ego led her to buy into their pitch without examining its fraudulent basis. Years ago women were forced to define themselves by their husbands' achievements because they were not allowed to strive for the same pinnacles. It was customary for a woman to defer to the man's need for education because the couple knew that he could make the most of it. So she would give up college in order to put him through whatever school he needed, secure in the knowledge that she would ultimately bask in the benefits of his status. But today the barriers are down and she has the opportunity to be whatever she wants and no longer must be consigned to a derivative existence.

Years ago a woman who wanted a career in medicine rarely dared to be a doctor but became a nurse; the women who longed to be a lawyer became a legal secretary. The only way to achieve a position of prestige was to marry it. The women who were strong enough to counter convention and pursue professional careers and sometimes chose to eschew the need for husbands were regarded as admirable but somewhat lacking because they were not wives and mothers. Marcia had swallowed this old line and as a result suffered from a sense of lost self-identity and could-have-been achievement. Everything in life is a tradeoff—but did she make the right one for her?

Marriage can be marvelous and singleness can be sensational. Millions of people live happily married lives and millions live happily unmarried lives. The difference between years ago and today, between then and now is the wonderful element of *choice* . . . choice when to marry, whom to marry and if to marry. No longer is there a need for a young woman to obsess because she is single and grab the guy who's available when panic strikes. She can now enjoy the luxury of evaluating the life-improving benefits offered by marriage and make a decision based on her needs rather than those of pressuring parents or conformist-demanding society. Secure in her own value as a person, plus the ability to support herself comfortably gives her the license to disregard the marriage license as the only acceptable route.

Unfortunately, many young women today profess to believe in the importance of what is called self-actualization and go so far as to pursue professional careers, but never manage to kick the conditioning that inculcated them with the belief that the only true arena of success for women is the home and that no matter what they accomplish elsewhere, they have failed as females unless they are married. Instead of revelling in the sense of satisfaction to which their achievements entitle them, they roil in self-doubt because they are single. Instead of enjoying the day to day pleasure derived from stimulating work activity, they denigrate its total importance as compared to the suddenly ennobling and unreachable state of matrimony and motherhood which they forget enmired their mothers in mediocrity and drudgery. They fought on the battlements for female equality and have earned parity positions that should bring them pride and pleasure. Instead, they read every daily wedding announcement with envy and suffer a sense of failure because their names are not there. Torn with jealousy over friends' marriages, they never bother to examine the often miserable realities of such existences as compared to their own. Never mind that one friend married into an emotional wasteland and another wed because of financial need. They got wedding rings, didn't they? And so these self-flagellants become obsessed with wedlock as a state of grace; they want to get married in the worst way and they do.

The Power of Negative Thinking

Paula is an attorney, the first in her family to go on to a higher degree. Pretty, with an engaging vitality, she has a highly responsible position in the estate department of a mid-sized law firm that pays her

$65,000 a year, which is more money than her father ever earned in his lifetime job with a utility company. She has her own apartment in a downtown neighborhood that is filled with young professionals, she shares rentals on a ski lodge in the winter and a beach house in the summer and takes Club Med vacations intermittently. Attractive and gregarious, finding men has never been a problem to Paula and she has had a succession of friendships, relationships, affairs and lived with a man for a year before they decided upon an amicable parting. Her job is stimulating, her life is busy and rewarding and she has the freedom of doing whatever she wants whenever she wishes, but an epiphany occurred when she reached thirty that suddenly destroyed any further possibility of enjoying her formerly totally satisfying existence.

"My God, I'm thirty and *not married*. Maybe I'll never get married. Maybe I'll be an old maid like poor Aunt Elsa and everyone will feel sorry for me. What am I doing? . . . I'd better find a *husband* fast."

Paula panicked and became an absolute neurotic on the subject until her friends became disgusted with both her conversation and behavior. She ran an ad in the "Personals" column of the local city magazine and met Bill, a pleasant unimaginative man of 36 who was also seeking a "meaningful relationship" and they started seeing each other steadily.

Bill was a classic JE, junior executive, who held a middle management job in a major consumer product corporation and thought that the epitome of ecstasy was to exceed last month's sales quota. Paula found

tisements of the local department store, all financed by low-interest loans offered by Paula's new employer. Her friends were hurt that she had left them out of such major moves, and annoyed by her haranguing accusations of their failures to keep in touch when it was actually *she* who had removed herself. They realized her anger was really a manifestation of self-reproach and that her long time reluctance to call was to defer facing their inevitable disapproval and disappointment with her. Each phone call ended with the promise of a future invitation to her new house . . . which they and she knew would never come.

*   *   *

Allowing yourself to be stampeded into marriage because of external forces rather than internal needs is foolish and can only have an unhappy ending. There is no reason today for any woman to "settle" for life with a husband she does not love and like. Given the fact that even when those elements are present there are no guarantees that the marriage will work, why further hamper your chances for success by starting with such a major handicap? In my book *The Seven Levels of Marriage: Expectations vs. Reality,* which takes you through the stages of maturation of a happy marriage, I describe the first "Entry Level" as one of the most difficult because it is the time when you both have to shake off your self-centered mind set and learn to accept the small to big annoyances of the ways and demands of another person. If there is not enough love and caring to sustain you during this period, it will be difficult to make the required effort. As I reiterated in this previous book, marriage can be wonderful. But not necessarily for everyone. To push into a marriage merely because you think it's time is to court disaster.

Stranded in Matrimony

Sally is a 33-year-old director of a nursery school day care center and last year completed her master's degree in education. She does not make a tremendous amount of money since the field is not a high-paying one, but she has always lived simply and has little desire for luxuries. Sally is very happy in her job, she loves working with children. Her small apartment is nicely furnished with pieces taken from her parents' house when they moved to Florida, and she shares it with Becky, a loveable floppy dog with the same placid disposition as her owner. Sally has a large network of good friends with whom she spends most evenings. Softspoken and slow moving, she exudes a calmness that is pleasant and somehow reassuring. She dislikes dating and prefers long term relationships like the one she had for two years with Jordan, a brash immature boy seven-years her junior who everyone was happy to see finally ejected from her home.

Even though Jordan's departure was her choice,

Sally missed his presence. Albeit irritating, he was someone. And she needed someone. Sally had no immediate family in the area and not much of one anywhere. Just after her parents moved to Florida, her father died, and her mother subsequently remarried. She had a disaffected brother who lived in Europe with whom she had no relationship at all. Sally was alone and longed for family; it was time to get married and create one. She began to notice an attractive man in her apartment building around whom she built a romantic mystique. Her friends shook their heads at Sally's almost teen-age obsession with this mystery man with whom she finally arranged a meeting. He was a free-lance industrial designer with the same laid-back personality as Sally and they started seeing each other. Ron was hard-working and forever weary. He would come over to her house ten o'clock at night after working all day and evening, and fall asleep on the floor watching TV.

Their relationship became steady, yet unlike romances where passion and need for each other pulls the partners together every waking moment, there were weeks when their sole contact was by phone because he was too busy or tired to see her. Her friends were puzzled by Sally's acceptance of Ron's absences and almost phlegmatic behavior when they were together and shocked when she told them that she intended to marry him. After a year of building his dependence on her for whatever small amount of female companionship he needed, she pulled the old squeeze play and announced that he must declare his serious intentions or she wanted out. She told him that she was thirty-three and wanted to get married and have children, and if he could not agree to those terms they were finished. In any "either/or" ultimatum, there is danger that the result won't be your choice. It's a risk that is easier to take when you do not have a heavy emotional investment in the outcome. Sally was sanguine because she knew that if it would not be Ron she would seek someone else; it was the moment and not the man that was all important. She won and they were wed three months later.

Upon Sally's advice, Ron gave up the uncertainty of free lancing and found a job with a design firm located in an outer suburb. Since Sally's master life plan included a house, they bought one in a town located fifty miles from the city but near Ron's office. Sally became pregnant almost immediately and continued to commute to her city job which involved almost two hours of convoluted connections of trains and buses. They both left early in the morning and she came home exhausted every evening and usually did not see Ron because either due to a tendency to disorganization or workaholism, he never seemed to make it out of the office until very late. His weekends were spent in the basement where he was building a studio to enable him to bring home unfinished work. Although they lived together, they seemed to be as separated as before their wedding. They saw so little of each other and talked so rarely that they had little chance to develop the understanding and intimacy that must be the basis of a happy and lasting relationship.

Sally had married because she wanted someone to share her life and yet now she found herself lonelier than ever before. Her friends were unwilling to make the big trek to her house so she rarely saw them. Her old pleasure of long chats on the phone was severely curtailed by Ron's carping at the size of their phone bills. She tried to find new friends and activities in the area but found they had made the major error of basing their decision to buy a house merely on the building without considering the neighborhood. It was a working class community of nice, solid people with whom she had absolutely nothing in common. She felt isolated and trapped, and longed to talk it over with her husband. Unfortunately, he wasn't there and the rare moments they had together involved financial discussions and his lectures on the need for economy in order to meet their growing responsibilities and expenses now that a child was on the way. She had always known that Ron was serious and heavy in his approach to life, but she hadn't realized what a drag it would be to live with someone with such a negative fearful view. One evening when they managed to have dinner together, she brought up the subject of names for their baby and began suggesting a few all of which he vetoed.

"How about Samuel? It's a nice name, it was my father's name."

"It's too Jewish," answered Ron.

Sally was stunned. Their religious difference had never seemed important and suddenly the fact that she was Jewish and he Protestant became an issue that could affect the attitudes and upbringing of their child.

"Who is this man I married?" she began to wonder and, "Can I spend the rest of my life with such a person?"

There are always doubts in the early stages of a marriage. It is the critical time when you learn to accept weaknesses and appreciate strengths. What gets you through is love and a subconscious balancing of the good and the bad. Sally loved Ron but it was not the overwhelming passion that either blinded her or compensated for the negatives of which there were many. However, the baby was imminent and that became the most important thing in her life.

After the birth of their son, Sally stayed home for a month and then resumed her old job, taking the baby with her. Working in a daycare center made it a natural since there were facilities for feeding, diapering and coping with an infant's needs. But the daily trip back and forth became even more onerous as she now carried a baby on her back. She adored her son but soon realized that he was her baby, not theirs. Ron took little interest in the child and regarded the infant as her total responsibility—that was woman's work.

When the baby was three months old, Ron suddenly announced that he had quit his job and taken a lease on his old studio back in the city which meant that he, too, would be commuting for three hours daily. Since he was starting a business, more time and dedication than ever would certainly be required.

Sally was heartsick. She had isolated herself in this stupid faraway house for his convenience and now he had negated the entire basis for her sacrifice. If there had been any glimmer of hope before that his workload would eventually ease up so that they could spend time together, this new move wiped out the possibility. The fact that he never considered consulting his wife before taking such a major career step was further proof to her that their concepts of love, sharing and parenthood were miles apart. When she entered the marriage she was ready to accommodate to Ron and expected the same consideration from him.

Going over their short marital history, she saw that he had given nothing to the relationship and was living exactly as he had when he was single with the added advantages of built-in maid and sex service. He had conceded to her pressure to marry because he had little to lose. She had made the down payment on the house with money she had inherited from her grandmother, so his investment was nil. She bore the baby and took full charge of him and Ron had the pleasures of a nice home and total domestic services. But what was in it for Sally? She felt betrayed; she felt sad; she felt stupid.

Sally was a victim of her own poor judgment. Perhaps she had been overly affected by the recent media hype about surveys that make a big to-do about women's diminishing chances for marriage and motherhood as the years roll on. What made age thirty-three the inviolate cut-off date that meant now or never for marriage? Why did she allow the sound of the ticking of the so-called biological clock to drown out the discordant noises from Ron that would have alerted her to his unsuitability as a husband? She wanted marriage because it seemed to present the pattern of life she desired. But was this a romantic vision or a real one? Her image of marriage was based on her family, her childhood, a split-level with mom in the kitchen and dad mowing the lawn. But these recollections were purely from a child's point of view. How much did she actually know about her mother's feelings? It never dawned upon her to consider whether her parents were happy, they were just there and married. Her father's retail business kept him busy days, evenings and Saturdays; wasn't her mother lonely? Did she like being married? Did her father fill her mother's needs and what were her needs anyway? Sally could not remember cross words between them, but then she didn't remember any words between them.

Sally had reached conclusions about marriage that were based on faulty research. Subconsciously she reasoned that marriage must be the only way to live, else why did her mother marry again after her father died? She should have realized that her mother had no other choice. That was her job title—wife— that's all she knew how to be and when she lost one job she just went out and found another. But Sally had options and did not have to accept emotional ne- glect and punitive living conditions. Her parents' arrangements where *he* gave at the office and *she* gave at home may have worked for them, but not for Sally.

If Sally had thought things through, she might

have realized that no longer is marriage the only lifestyle available to women; all sorts of satisfactory household arrangements exist that proclaim societal attitudes of incredible laissez-faire.

Sally wanted a home and child, and she actually provided both for herself. As she learned, there's more to fathering than fertilization and having a man around the house doesn't always mean companionship. Unmarried motherhood might have been a viable alternative for Sally. Isn't she actually functioning as a single parent anyway?

Attitudes ARE Changing

Today's woman is having second thoughts about the cliche that we must be married and that it is the only possible consummation of a relationship between a man and woman. A recent episode of the hit television show "Cagney and Lacey" was devoted to Chris Cagney's rejection of a marriage proposal from her long-time lover. In the not-so-olden days his "will you marry me?" would have broken down her resolve for independence which after all was probably just a pose because what real woman wants to stay single, and the program would have ended with a beautiful wedding with not a dry eye in the house. Instead, her answer was "no." The reasons?

"Why can't we just go on seeing each other because we want to, not because we have to?"

When he tells her he wants to share a life with her, she counters with "But that will be your life we'll be sharing, not mine." She goes on to utter other heretofore heretical statements about women's attitudes toward marriage today.

"I don't know if I ever wanted marriage. But if I did, the dream is gone now. There are moments when knowing that I won't have a child is an ache, but most of the time I don't feel that way. I like my life just as it is."

The program concludes with her happily married partner commending Chris for making the choice that is obviously right for her. Says she: "Seeing you married to David and visiting you with a houseful of kids would make me happy, yes, but that's my fantasy. This is your deal."

True, this is only a dramatist's dialogue, but TV is a medium that is renowned for lack of courage in taking positions and for its pandering to the sensibilities and sensitivities of the masses. Thus, when a major television series portrays a beautiful desirable woman making the choice to never marry, you know that in 1988 non-marriage has become a recognized and acceptable lifestyle choice for women everywhere.

SEVEN

Why Divorced Women with Kids Shouldn't Marry

The absurd is essentially a divorce.
—ALBERT CAMUS

"I KNEW I SHOULDN'T INTERFERE—but when I heard Alan yelling at Michelle, I couldn't stand it. He may be my husband, but he's not her father."

Those kinds of conflicts inevitably occur when

the man of the house isn't the father of the resident children; clashes become corrosive and divided loyalties tear a woman apart. Is it worth it?

The process of divorce in itself is painful and destructive to everyone involved, mother, father and children. When the legalities are completed, the wife can buckle down to the task of rebuilding a family life for herself and the children with the new lineup of single parent authority. It's a big adjustment for everyone but, in time, things settle into an acceptable routine. The kids find their lives in school and with friends go on much the same. Even though they now see dad on alternate weekends only, the stability of having mom always there keeps them on an even keel. Before long, the divorce that at first seemed to be a horrible, revolutionary eruption now becomes just another accepted element. After all, lots of kids in school have divorced parents, what's the big deal? In fact, it's kind of nice to have mom all to one's self and not have to share her with dad who was always resentful when she spent the evening helping a hysterical daughter with her term paper ("Help me, Mom. I'm gonna fail, I know it!") leaving him alone in front of the TV set, or angry when she interrupted his pre-prandial cocktail hour to run out and pick up a son after choir practice ("Why don't you let him walk home or ride his bike? So what if it's raining, he won't melt"). And for sure, no one's going to miss the constant bickering and fighting that made the house a misery at times. It's really not too bad; having two homes gets to seem natural after a while.

But what about mom? After the initial relief over

the cessation of hostilities, and the residual bitterness fades, going to bed alone every night and having no adult at home to share the tales of the day with creates a void that needs filling. So she starts dating. At first, the kids are discomforted by the presence of a courting male. Mothers shouldn't have boyfriends, teenagers have boyfriends, babysitters have boyfriends. But mom, it's weird. Then they get used to her going out to dinner, or wherever couples go in the evenings. In time, they become accustomed to the presence of different men. Increasingly, one man seems to be in the house more often and they sort of get used to having him around. He's not their father, but he's O.K. He doesn't bother them, in fact, he tries to be very nice to them, and mom seems to be happier.

Then mom calls the kids together in the living room and tells them that she and what's his name are getting married. Suddenly they have to face a new eruption. Just when they had adjusted to all the arrangements and convoluted time-sharing confusion that divorced parents create, a new divisive element is being introduced and they will have to face coping with another person whose status is a puzzlement and whose presence has already changed mom's response to their needs. They are upset, they are scared, they hate it and though he seems like a nice guy, they hate him a little, too.

This is the atmosphere in which the new marriage gets its start. And if you think the kids' initial antagonism is difficult, wait until the new man moves in.

Two Homes
Can Be Better Than One

Rita met Martin at a "Parents Without Partners" meeting. It was two years after a very messy and acrimonious divorce from a neurotic husband who had driven her crazy with demands for attention and rules for behavior that had kept her and her two little daughters in a state of constant turmoil. He had categorically refused to leave their comfortable suburban house until she was driven to take the children and move into an apartment in the area. Although this was against the advice of her attorney, it was encouraged by her therapist who knew Rita would crack up if she continued to live with that maniac. The little girls, aged 10 and 12, missed their friends and neighborhood and the space of their own rooms and a large house, but were soon happy to be free of the erratic tirades from a father who demanded neatness and order. And they did have the stability of continuing in the same school.

Rita's job as trust officer for a local bank was interesting and responsible and she resumed the active social life network with her childhood friends and relatives whom she had been unable to see during her marriage because of her husband's cantankerous refusal to have anything to do with her family. She missed sex, however, and desired the company of men. So when she heard of this group of people in similar circumstances, she attended a meeting and met Martin who had recently divorced his wife of twenty-two years.

Rita was forty-one, which was fifteen years younger than Martin. He was the manager of a large local hardware store and like Rita, had lived in the area all of his life. He, too, had two children but they were in their twenties and off on their own. Rita was a very controlled, self-contained woman and she found herself attracted to Martin's outgoing personality and highly emotional reactions to almost everything. Where she cared only about selected people, institutions and events, he cared about everything and everybody and was forever exploding at one of his children's behavior or inveighing against the activities of the government and writing irate letters to the local newspapers. Like most people who hate deeply, he also loved deeply and his warmth and affection were a delightful change to Rita who had been living with an icy husband who had difficulty even saying "Have a nice day." They started dating and her daughters became accustomed to seeing Martin in and out of the house. On weekends when the girls were with their father, Rita and Martin went off to nearby inns, or he stayed over at her apartment and just lazed around and enjoyed sex and the Sunday papers.

Then he asked her to marry him. Rita was hesitant because things were very pleasant and right for her now. Furthermore, from her experience with marriage, she did not see where becoming husband and wife would improve the situation. In fact, she had serious reservations about the many possibilities for wreaking havoc on what was a comparatively smooth and carefree life. But Martin was persistent.

Why not? From where he sat, marriage would be a major upgrade. Rita had a home and family. He, on the other hand, lived alone in a small apartment which was all he could afford after alimony payments. A lifetime of wifely care had made him totally unfamiliar with the kitchen or washing machine and taking care of his basic living needs presented daily problems. A gregarious man with no real interest other than his work and attending the movies, plays and dinner parties his wife had arranged for, the solitary life was not for him. He was lost and needed the structure and company supplied by a wife.

He pleaded and cajoled and Rita began to waver. Her first response to his proposal was a resounding no, but Martin's continuous persuasion began to have its effect. His arguments plus the niggling fear that her refusal would ultimately turn him off and lead him to look elsewhere finally made her agree. And so they were married, and Martin happily moved into Rita's bedroom and prepared to perform the role as husband and stepfather.

The first rude awakening came in front of the TV set, a place Martin loved to spend his evenings. When the girls wanted to turn on their favorite programs, he insisted on watching wrestling or "Hill Street Blues." Since there was but one set in the house and it was located smack in the middle of the living room, his positioning himself there with the blasting sound he preferred became a major irritant for the entire household. When he walked in one afternoon after school and found them watching a soap opera, he turned off the set in a fury because they

124

should not at their ages be allowed to see the sort of licentious activities that abound on the tube at teatime, and their mother was wrong to be so permissive. It was one battle after another. The conflicts of interest and opinion were bad enough, but even worse was the highly emotional yelling that was Martin's natural response to anything of which he disapproved. This was frightening to the girls who were used to the cold silences and tight-lipped castigations of their father, and made them confused and angry. After all, who did he think he was anyway? He wasn't their father, he was an interloper who had insinuated himself into their home and was trying to take over. The purchase of another TV set for the girls' room helped somewhat, but his continual presence and vocal opinions on their behavior made the home unpleasant. Since Martin's store was just a few blocks from the apartment, he was home early and dropped in frequently and the girls felt their lives were being destroyed by this man who always had something to say about everything they did.

Rita used to look forward to coming home after a day at the bank and relaxing with the girls at the kitchen table with a pot of tea while they regaled her with the details of their days' activities. It was a warm, happy time—but now it was destroyed. Instead, she felt she was entering a war zone when she opened the front door. The girls were either sulking in their rooms or worse, were away studying at friends' houses because they hated their own. Martin was usually ensconced in front of the TV ready to greet her angrily with complaints about her daughters' disrespectful behavior.

"What did I need this for?" she wondered as she sat up at night unable to sleep after another bedtime disagreement with Martin about her performance as a wife and mother. Martin was of another generation and his approach to child rearing was totally different than Rita's. Also, he had sons and regarded daughters as vestal-virgins-in-training who had to be guided and protected from heaven knows what. Mothering is difficult enough when fraught with the dual guilt of divorce and career; the constant carping of a critic begins to undermine self-confidence and can turn even the firmest parent into a vacillating wimp. Rita began to question everything she thought and did and found herself unable to make even the simplest decisions about the children.

Torn between responsibility to her daughters and to her husband, she began to feel that the good new life she had fought so hard to achieve for herself and her children was in jeopardy. Rita's divorce had been a bitter battle with a vindictive husband. In order to create a stable, happy home for herself and her daughters, she had willingly sacrificed the comfort and security of a well-subsidized life that included a luxurious five-bedroom house and live-in maid, moved to an apartment that was half the size of her house and went to work. To see everything she had hard won collapsing because of Martin made her wonder if she had not made a terrible mistake.

Rita loved Martin and was truly reluctant to give up on their marriage, but she saw no way that their lives could continue under the present arrangement without doing damage to the carefully constructed happy new life she and her children had just begun to enjoy. The constant friction among them was destroying her relationship with the girls as well as her love for Martin. Her anger over being forced into the no-win role as referee was changing her from a serene person into an irritable neurotic. Finally she realized that she had left one kind of destructive marriage only to enter into another. But there was one major difference. Her first husband was an erratic, oppressive person with whom she could never spend her entire life. But Martin was a kind, loving man who she knew could make her happy, and the relationship was definitely worth saving. If only she hadn't permitted herself to be talked into marriage. She finally came up with what she considered a workable solution and bided her time for the right moment to broach it to her husband.

She waited until the girls were out visiting friends one Friday evening, and then sat Martin down in the living room and presented him with a stunning proposition.

She told him that there was no longer any viable possibility that their marriage could survive under the existing conflicted conditions. Even if they moved to a house which might alleviate some of the concentrated intimacy enforced by the close proximity of an apartment, it would not change the rigid stepfather stance Martin had unfortunately assumed. Nor would it alter the fact that he did not approve of her children, and she did not approve of his disapproval. Rita told him that she considered him a wonderful guy and lover, but his flareups and explosions over even small domestic problems had brought a disruptive note into what had heretofore been a placid and happy household.

"I don't want to break up, Martin. I do love you, but I don't know how much longer I will if we keep on this way. I keep thinking about how wonderful it was before. Do you remember how we enjoyed our weekends, what fun we had, how we laughed over dinner? Now all we ever do is argue.

"What I want us to do in order to save our marriage is to go back to living like before. You move back to your apartment, and we'll spend weekends together like before. We'll go out to dinner and places some evenings during the week. But you won't live here. Bring me your laundry, that's fine. You'll even eat over an evening or two during the week the way you used to. You'll always have the comfort and security of knowing that you have a wife to love you, depend upon, to take care of you when you get sick. Look, I know it sounds crazy but I think it will work. Some people have separate bedrooms, we'll have separate apartments. Think about it, when the girls are racing around here blasting their radios, or bringing in friends who take over the kitchen, rummage around the fridge and make popcorn, don't you sometimes really wish you were back in your old nice quiet apartment? Face it, you're 56 and have no patience with young kids. Maybe in eight years or so when the girls are in college, we'll live under one roof. But right now, we can do everything together just like a married couple except live together."

After Martin's initial shock wore off, he began to view the proposal calmly. He loved Rita and did not want to give her up. He, too, had come to realize that their life was becoming untenable but had avoided facing up to the dread alternative. If they broke up, they would have only a past. But if he accepted Rita's proposal, they could have a pleasant present and a certain future. Martin moved back to his old apartment and they started an entirely new living arrangement which turned out to be not only highly satisfactory, but a little exciting as well.

The concept of two-home relationships is more common than might be imagined. Many women want to preserve their privacy and independence yet want the comfort and reassurance of a dependable ongoing relationship. And why not? It's your life and whatever arrangements work for you and your partner are acceptable today. Some people may consider your lifestyle remarkable, but there are many who will regard it as enviable.

Illicit
Is Now Licit

Audrey is a college professor who lived in the suburbs with her husband and two teenage sons when she had an affair with her next door neighbor, Mark who was also married with children. Mark's wife was ill and he did not want to leave her. When she died, and his daughters were in college, he moved to an apartment in the city. Shortly thereafter, Audrey divorced her husband and moved to an apartment in Mark's building.

In no way did Audrey ever again wish to tie her life to a man. She wanted a place for her sons to live during school holidays, where they would feel totally comfortable and at home without the disturbing presence of an outsider who would necessarily have some quasi authority over their behavior. She did not want to have to deal with a man's needs, demands and raging id. She wanted a man, she wanted Mark—but not twenty-four hours a day. She wanted to be able to come home from a particularly exhausting day and head for the martini pitcher and a bath without saying a word for two hours, and not have to face the hangdog look of the hurt husband or rejected resident male. She wanted to spend some evenings and nights with Mark but not necessarily all of them.

This was ten years ago and the relationship still flourishes. Friends regard them as a couple and usually invite them together. Mark's daughters know that Audrey is their father's lover and her sons are aware of the setup as well. But nobody minds because the relationship in no way inhibits the children's access to their parents, as it would if they shared habitation. In fact, the children are happy that their parents are happy and not alone, thus less of a responsibility. It's the perfect solution because it works for everyone concerned.

Years ago such a relationship would have been regarded as scandalously illicit and all family members would pretend it did not exist. My grandmother's younger sister had a husband with whom she lived during the week and a lover she saw over the weekends, an arrangement that went on for more than twenty years with the closed-eye awareness of the entire family. This bizarre setup evolved from the fact that in the early 1900's people were poor and two families frequently shared lodgings in order to reduce their rents. When Uncle Benjie's sister and her husband Daniel and two little sons moved in with him and my great aunt Libby and their children, no one envisioned that Libby and Daniel would fall madly in love and actually have a torrid affair that drove Uncle Benjie's wife to suicide. I remember Aunt Libby as a nice looking lady who lived in the Bronx and was a wonderful cook, but somehow I could not reconcile the lurid image of seductress with a woman who made sensational noodle pudding. But obviously under that Swirl housedress was a body that drove men wild because cuckolded Uncle Benjie refused to give her up and newly widowed Daniel maintained that he could not live without her. Thus, they came to an arrangement that worked for them until the men died and Libby lived on until the ripe age of ninety-two.

I have always hated the words "working at a marriage" because the term conveys a duty and drudgery that detracts from the pleasure marriage should provide for those who choose it. But non-marriage relationships often require a certain amount of planning and effort because there are more factors that have to be considered and meshed in order to make them run smoothly and satisfactorily for all concerned.

The Right Lover
Often the Wrong Stepfather

Constance is a handsome blond divorcee of thirty-eight who lives in a very small town in Vermont with her two sons aged thirteen and fifteen. She is an extremely successful saleswoman for a land sale company that sells dreams to city folk who long to own a piece of peaceful pastoral respite from the rat-race. Her income from commissions last year was $85,000, and this year looks even better.

She owns a nice house that is run efficiently and happily by a local woman who takes care of the boys, sees that they have milk and home-made cookies when they come home from school, usually with a pack of friends, and a hot and nutritious dinner every night. Constance never has dinner with her sons. She is usually too exhausted after a day's work to deal with the rowdy rambunctiousness of teenagers and the boys are too busy with their friends to want to talk to her anyway. She eats out every night and comes home about 8:00 to help with homework and hear about the boys' day. It's an arrangement that may seem strange to some but has worked out wonderfully. The boys are active, happy and doing well in school and Constance is able to pursue her own life and career without the distracting and destructive onus of guilt.

The choice of that house in that town was carefully planned. When her divorce from a ne'er-do-well husband was final, she was left with two small boys and little chance of collecting child support from a man who never held a job longer than six months. Knowing that she would be the sole support of the family, she looked for a career where income was contingent upon input effort because she knew she had the drive and brains to succeed. When she was offered a selling job with the land company where acreage units went for five figures and up and thus earned commissions could become sizeable, she knew this was exactly the opportunity she sought.

Fully aware that tremendous amounts of time and energy would have to be devoted to the job in order to produce, she went about making proper provisions for the care and upbringing of her boys. Because she knew she would have to be absent a good deal, she sought and found a small town where neighbors become extended families and front doors are always welcomingly open. Using her total savings, she bought a small house smack in the middle of town so that they would be surrounded by people and activities. And then she found a local woman who was eager to earn a comparatively easy income caring for two boys who were at school all day and a house with no critical madam white-gloving the woodwork.

Constance's well-thought-out plan gave her and her children the kind of solid secure existence and future she wanted for them. A vital and attractive woman, she had needs for sex and male companionship which she found with not too much difficulty. The only shadow in what was an otherwise highly satisfactory and happy life was the continually expressed disapproval of her puritanic Scottish-born mother who lived in another state but still managed to use the telephone, mails and frequent visits to comment on her daughter's hedonistic life of sin.

"A woman should be married. Divorcing your husband was bad enough. True he was a wastrel but a good woman could have made something from him. You failed at marriage, and now you are failing as a mother. Leaving those boys alone all day in the care of strangers! They need a mother and a father."

It was a constant litany that annoyed but did not bruise Constance. Although most of us seek our parents' approval until the day they or we die, Constance had lost respect for her mother's opinions when she was ten years old and received what she considered an asinine answer to the question of who was the "They" who seemed to control the family's behavior. Constance had wanted to wear her new patent leather Mary Jane pumps, but her mother forbid it because "They" did not wear patent leather until Easter. When her mother could not identify or even describe this all-powerful "They" who were the major force in decisions about what was important, wrong or right, Constance decided that her mother was a silly woman and never really listened to her again.

Constance dated a number of men until she met Roger, a widower with no children, who became her steady companion. He owned a thriving, prosperous construction company which he had built from scratch in a field noted for toughness and power. A strong-minded and opinionated man, Constance rather enjoyed his firm unilateral decision-making

that enabled her to coast along mindlessly in her social life in happy contrast to the stressful problem-
solving requirements of her business life. One week-
end he announced they were flying to the Bahamas
and they did. Another time it was a ski chalet. He
was great fun, good company and the sex was marvelous. He picked her up at home from time to time
and got to know her sons. Constance was amused at
his tough guy dealings with the boys and what she
jokingly referred to as his "construction crew boss"
posture.

Her mother met Roger and was tremendously
impressed with him.

"Now there's a fine real man. He'd make a wonderful husband for you and father to the boys. You'd
better try to get him to marry you because Lord
knows you're not getting any younger and with two
sons, who knows when you'll get another chance. A
handsome man like that and rich too, I wonder he
sees anything in you at all what with all the pretty
young girls he could probably get."

Constance began to spend a good deal of time
with Roger in the lavish apartment he maintained in a
nearby city and their life settled into a pleasant and
almost domesticated existence. One day he told
Constance he had decided that it was time that they
got married.

"You decided?" said Constance laughing. "How
about asking me?"

Roger shrugged since he considered proposing
only a foolish formality that would naturally elicit a
"yes" answer.

"No," said Constance. "I don't want to get married. I did that already and it's not for me."

Roger was absolutely shocked. The possibility of refusal had never entered his mind.

"What you did before has nothing to do with now," he said. "Your husband was a loser and good-riddance. I'd give you a good life and be a father to your kids."

She looked at him in surprise. "But we have a good life just as it is. And I don't want a stepfather for my sons. Why don't we just keep things as they are?"

Roger was furious. Here he had finally made the big concession and decision to make a major commitment, and he was rebuffed. It was unthinkable. Then he gave Constance an ultimatum.

"I want to get married. I want a home and a wife. So either you say 'yes' or that's it and we stop seeing each other. Think it over. You'll come to your senses. Don't give me your answer now; save it for next week."

The next time her mother dropped in for a visit, she noticed that her daughter was no longer seeing Roger.

"So he threw you over, did he? Didn't want to marry you, of course, just as I thought. Men! They're all the same."

Constance never bothered to tell her mother that in no way would she ever have considered bringing Roger into her home. He was a fun guy to visit but she would never subject her sons to his authoritative demands. She could cope with his bullying ways, but her young sons could not. She would have been perfectly content continuing the lifestyle pattern they

years ago and walked out with her two-year-old son and infant daughter on a marriage that she felt was a dreadful mistake. Helped by minimal child support payments, she worked as a saleswoman in a neighborhood clothing store where her children could stop in on the way home from school and visit with her for a few minutes before going home to the apartment which was just a few doors down. Carl was a machinist in a local plant and they had been dating for a few months and now felt their relationship was ready to move on into a more serious commitment.

Vicki was thirty-seven and Carl was the same age and had never been married. He liked her children, loved her, and had a pleasant easy-going disposition that Vicki felt would make him a welcome addition to the household. He mentioned marriage but Vicki ignored it.

"OK," she told him. "You move in and let's see how it works out. But remember this, you're my friend, your relationship is strictly with me and not the kids. You're not their father, you're not their boss. Only I am. If they do something that bugs you, tell me and I'll deal with it. They've been brought up to respect grown-ups so they'll be good kids. So it should all work out fine."

And it did. Relieved of the need to assert a position with the children, he just relaxed and they began to accept him, at first as a nice friend and then as someone to respect and admire whose judgment they sought constantly to the delight of their mother. Rather than having to force his authority upon them, he earned the right to impose it in time. Five years later, they have developed a warm relationship that is totally undistinguishable from any conventional nuclear family. From time to time, Vicki is asked why she and Carl do not marry.

"What for?" she says. "How will that make it better?"

In an article that appeared in the February 15, 1988, issue of *People* magazine, Priscilla Presley was asked the same question about her relationship with the man whose child she had just borne and who had been living with her and her teen-age daughter.

"We've both been married before and we both feel that a marriage contract doesn't make it any better or worse. Marriage is somewhat of a business and as of now our relationship is not a business."

EIGHT

Why Widows Shouldn't Marry: You've Been Through Enough

> Take care! Kingdoms are destroyed by bandits, houses by rats, and widows by suitors.
> —*The Japanese Family Storehouse,*
> by Ihara Saikaku, 1683

THE WORD "WIDOW" carries a past of pain.

Whether her husband died shockingly suddenly or agonizingly slowly, a widow has undergone insupportable anguish from which, in some sense, she will never totally recover. The experience affects different women in different ways and creates behavioral responses that are often unexpected. One response, however, that every widow can expect almost immediately from friends, acquaintances and relatives will be a prediction, which is probably meant to be a mix of comfort and flattery. In reality, it is actually insensitive and offensive.

"Mark my words, you'll remarry, and sooner than you think."

It is incredible how normally considerate and kindly people feel that the loss of a woman's husband permits them to enter her bedroom and private life with advice and intimate questions that they would never think of discussing were she married. Tasteless questions about her "love life" and unsolicited guidance on how to proceed with the search for a new mate, which everyone assumes is the goal of every widow, laced with dire warnings about the shortage of eligible men are the common topics of conversation.

Everybody's a maven in the matrimonial marketplace. If she had a good marriage, the popular position will be that she'll want to replicate the situation as fast as possible. If she had a miserable marital relationship, then naturally now she will want to wipe out the disastrous past by making a happy and satisfactory union. In any case, everybody has the reason why she must immediately embark upon a concerted drive to *find a new husband*.

No one bothers to think about what the widow has begun to think about. Which is—"Why the hell should I ever want to remarry?'' Why indeed. Other than completing the couple symmetry of friends' dinner tables, why does she have to be half of a team to be socially acceptable? And if she must take a partner with her on social occasions, why does he have to be a spouse?

Remarriage is no longer the knee-jerk response of widows. Today there are alternative lifestyles available to women that allow them to evaluate all the elements of reentering matrimony and make judgments based upon emotional rather than societal demands.

You Can't Recreate the Past. Why Complicate Your Future?

Joan's husband of twenty-seven years had a massive coronary on the tennis court in the middle of their regular Sunday morning doubles game. Despite the immediate ministrations of physicians on adjacent courts, he died before reaching the hospital. Although he was overweight, with a gourmand appetite that leaned heavily towards fourteen-ounce steaks and side orders of garlic bread, coupled with working in the high stress advertising field, he had a perfect health history and literally had never been sick a day in their life.

Joan was an intelligent capable woman who worked as a psychologist for the local school system but nothing had prepared her for the sudden loss of the man she had loved and fully expected to live with for at least another twenty to thirty years. Surrounded by her children and friends, she went through all the details and rituals of the funeral with the calm competence everyone expected from her. Almost immediately thereafter, she sold their house and moved into a nearby apartment. Concerned friends were happy to notice that she was going out and keeping busy and adjusting well to her tragic loss. What no one realized was just how much she was going out and why. For that first year, Joan went someplace, any place, virtually every evening after work in order to avoid facing the empty apartment. As time passed and she looked back over that period, Joan realized she remembered nothing of the first six months after her husband's death. Although her calm allayed the concerns of friends, her deceptive demeanor was merely a coverup for the fact that she was in shock.

It took Joan another year to recover and reconcile herself to the fact that her husband was gone and the life she had taken for granted was over. At that point she began to rebuild her existence and plan for the future. Remarriage was not part of it. What for? There were strong reasons for her marrying twenty-eight years ago, none of which applied now.

Then she was a young girl living at home with her parents, awaiting the arrival of Mr. Right who would carry her off and give her a home, family, security and a properly married place in society. She had all that now, plus the immense personal satisfaction of a successful career.

What could a husband add to her life at this point except complication, conflict and compromise? When you live with a man for many years, including those young formative ones when flexibility plus passion make it easier to adapt to each other's wishes, you develop a communion of tastes and attitudes that makes your day to day living comfortable and predictable. You know what to expect from each other in almost all situations because you have been through it before. Remarriage at a mature stage in life means adapting to someone whose habits you had no part in formulating, whose reactions to familiar situations will be totally unfamiliar and potentially unpleasant.

Think of all the life experiences, major and minor, that married couples encounter together for the first time to which they form a joint reaction that anneals into permanent attitudes and habits. Maybe it was that first trip to Europe when their introduction to the continental luxury of breakfast in the room developed into their thenceforth automatic hotel routine. Or when they started preparing meals together and found they both hated facing a sinkful of pots and dishes after a satisfying meal, which got them into the technique of keeping food warm on the hottray while a pre-prandial cleanup was effected. Everyday life is filled with these little idiosyncrasies that become basic habits and make it more difficult to adapt to living with another person who does not share or even understand them. And the older we get, the more difficult it is to change or compromise.

My widowed mother remarried a lovely man who unintentionally terrorized her with complaints about her cooking because she did not use the spices to which he was accustomed. He badgered her until she became almost paralyzed with uncertainty at the stove she had worked over for fifty years. With great difficulty, she finally learned how to prepare food to please him.

Women are used to being the ones called upon to make the compromises. In the *Time* magazine October 12, 1987, cover story "Are Women Fed Up?" E. James Lieberman, a Washington psychiatrist who specializes in couples therapy, observed, "Women are still giving more than they get."

In her article in *The New York Times* "Hers" column of January 9, 1986, Katha Pollitt says, "Both sexes have been socialized to see relationship-maintenance as primarily a woman's responsibility. . . . We live in a society that drums into women's heads from the minute they're born that they are here on earth to play supporting roles in essentially male dramas. Marriage has traditionally been one such drama, but so is American culture itself."

If Joan were to remarry, she would have to remake her life over in the image of the man she married. His needs would have to be met, and for many reasons, men seem to have more needs than women. It does not require reading of feminist tracts to become aware of the inflated sense of male entitlement that has been nurtured by families and society. Men are brought up with the implicit expectation of being served by women. The tendency for this self-importance to develop into intractability is reinforced in the workplace where observation of rules and restrictions are inherent in daily operations causing men to develop a rigid code of behavior. Women on the other hand, have been raised and socialized to be accommodating. Add this basic wish to please to the fact that they function in the freer world of home where momentary feelings and emotions are permitted to govern responses to situations, and it is apparent why women develop the better ability to adapt and cope with change.

Joan was a woman who did not like to be alone. Or so she thought. She had always enjoyed coming home and getting dinner started in anticipation of her husband's hour-later arrival when they would have drinks and discuss their day's activities. It was a warm, pleasant ritual because it was held against the background of a shared lifetime of interests and concerns. Conversations involved their children, their careers that both had helped each other build, relatives and familiar family feuds. There was no way Joan could ever expect to duplicate those exchanges with a man with whom she would have only the most recent frames of reference. If she remarried she might reproduce the situation but never the elements that gave it value.

Joan opted to not remarry and announced her decision to all who would listen. But no one believed her. It is just another one of those double-standard devilments that beset women forever that a widower's statement of reluctance to remarry is accepted instantly whereas a widow's is viewed as a coverup for her undesirability. And this skewed reaction does not come from men only.

The Pleasures of the Single Life

Right after Doris' husband died suddenly of a heart attack, her widowed friends rallied around to console and comfort her.

"Give yourself a chance to settle into a single life before you make any big changes. You may not ever want to remarry, we don't."

Doris did not believe them. How could a woman prefer to live without a husband? Although at fifty-three, she had a career as a merchandise manager that she had resumed when her two sons were grown, she was very dependent upon her husband for handling the finances and making the major decisions in their lives. She felt lost, lonely and in limbo without him and assumed all other women felt the same.

"Poor things, they can't find husbands," Doris thought about her widowed friends. "It's just sour grapes when they say they're not looking to get married again."

With the help of her sons, Doris sold her suburban home and bought an apartment in the city near her office and became enthusiastic and excited about her new neighborhood and lifestyle. Many evenings she walked home from work and thoroughly enjoyed exploring and discovering small tucked away shops and details of architectural elegance that she had never before noticed. She found satisfaction in handling the details of her life and began to appreciate the absence of pressures imposed by dependence. No longer did she have to watch the clock nervously and feel the pull to notify her husband that she might be late. If she came across an interesting restaurant on her way home, there was nothing to stop her from having dinner on impulse without having to contend with a balking husband who was never adventurous when it came to food. And when her department required a buying trip to the Orient, she did not have to pass up the opportunity because her husband refused to be alone for so long a period. Now she went freely and had a marvelous time.

Doris began to appreciate aloneness. There was a quiet peace in her apartment that she grew to love. She had plenty of activity at her office, and interaction with people all day long. She looked forward to her home as a comfortable retreat and respite from the hectic business world. To give her life the structure most of us require, Doris began to develop a routine and like all widows, began to discover how much of her married life had been devoted to the demands and desires of her husband. As she created little rituals designed to please only herself, she realized how much of what and when she ate, what she bought, what she wore, what TV programs she watched, even what books she read, had been influenced by her husband's desires and opinions. Even though he was not overbearing, or tyrannical, he managed in his own gentle way to make his likes and dislikes apparent. And being a woman and wife who was trained to please, she had tailored her activities, behavior and the running of the household to suit him.

Little by little, the liberation process evolved as

Doris bought the beautiful wide-brimmed hat that she hadn't permitted herself since the time her husband said she was too short for a big hat and it made her look like a mushroom. Next she broke out into buying clothes in the bright colors she loved but had eschewed in favor of the subdued tans and grays her husband preferred. She started cooking with abandon, experimenting with new recipes containing the many exotic spices available in her new neighborhood, without fear of incurring disapproval from a husband who preferred simple foods and regarded all dishes that were unfamiliar to be inedible. She bought a subscription to the ballet instead of the once in a while performances that she sometimes managed to drag her grumbling spouse to attend.

As Doris began to expose herself to more and more new experiences, she realized how much of herself she had subconsciously suppressed over the years in order to make her husband happy and to avoid conflict. In a longtime marital relationship, each person is changed by the attitudes of the other often to the point of radical transformation. These altering forces frequently work to the partner's benefit as in the cases of those who blossom into confident attractive individuals with new positive images of themselves derived from the admiration of spouses. Many develop courage to achieve instilled by their mates' supportive belief and encouragement. But more often the changes effected by the dynamics of living together are less dramatic and result in subtle restraints and behavior modifications that in time become imperceptible because they seem built in. It is only when the strictures are removed that the surviving spouse becomes aware of how much of herself she has sacrificed for peace and a way of life she valued—at the time.

But at this point in time, what does marriage offer? Doris was now a different person. She flourished in her new free life and discovered the joys and satisfactions of independence. When she needed advice about financial matters, once handled totally by her husband, she conferred with her sons and made her own decisions helped but not bound by their suggestions. True, she often missed the loving relationship she had with her husband, and felt sad knowing it could never be again. But having sons whom she could depend upon to care for and love her did much to fill the void.

Then she met Lewis, a sixty-year-old widower, who was an accountant in an adjacent office. They started dating casually at first, and soon found they were spending all their leisure time together. Within a few months, it developed into an intimate and relaxed relationship that became important to both of them. Most weekends he slept at her house, and they took vacation trips together. But when he went home, as he always did, to his apartment which was about a half-hour's drive from hers, she found she liked his leaving. A year went by and one of her co-workers asked her when she and Lewis were getting married.

"Married?" said Doris. "But I don't want to get married." And then she saw the questioner's skeptical smile and suddenly thought "My God, she doesn't believe me." She remembered her own incredulity at similar expressions from her widowed friends. But now she knew they were telling the truth because she would never consider marrying Lewis, even though she loved him. She had come to treasure her independence and freedom and was proud of the highly satisfactory life she had carefully constructed that enabled her to pursue every avenue of interest to her, without restriction. She liked to wake up in bed next to Lewis, sometimes. She liked to spend evenings and days with Lewis, sometimes. She liked to be with Lewis because she wanted to be, not because she had to be. She liked when he arrived and she liked when he left and she could close her door and return to the total privacy of her home. She liked to be free, and she knew she would never, never marry.

When my husband died and people, who shouldn't have, asked me if I planned to remarry, my answer was always "Never." It's a simple definitive word but few seemed to understand it. "You mean right now, it's 'never.' " "No," I said, "Always it's never."

I was happily married for thirty-five years in an era when marriage was the only socially acceptable lifestyle. It was happy, companionable and loving replete with all the proverbial ups and downs expected in a long-term relationship. But it ended with the worst possible "down" to be encountered in marriage, the severe and ultimately fatal illness of a mate. Which is one big reason why I and millions of other widows past middle age will not remarry, ever.

The Job Description
Reads "Nurse"

Consider the potential husbands for women in their late forties, fifties, sixties and older: men in their fifties, sixties and older who are candidates for heart attacks, strokes and all the other health disasters that occur with alarming frequency in men of these ages. When you marry young and years later your husband becomes ill and/or incapacitated, you love him and care for him willingly. You married for better or worse and this is the worse. It is the fair and equitable price for the many years of health and happiness that you shared. But to marry a fifty-or-over man who is just entering the high risk health years is courting disaster and the job description reads "nurse."

Twice when I attended funerals of men who had died suddenly I found myself in the sobbing arms of their grieving wives who said to me through tears "At least you were able to be prepared when David died. For me it's such a horrible shock."

I forgave them for the imbecility of their statements and wrote it off to the unbalancing effect of bereavement. They were, in effect, telling me how lucky I was to have had four years of illness and deterioration to ready myself for the ultimate end. I would have liked to tell them that no matter how often you face the possibility of an ill loved one's death, nothing in the world can prepare you for the utter desolation of defeat over losing a long-fought battle or for the numbing sense of finality of the death itself.

Unless you have lived through the anguish of watching a person you love undergo pain, agony, fear and disintegration you cannot possibly comprehend the utter despair and hopelessness that pervades every waking moment of your life. When I see an elderly woman in an airport, restaurant, or museum pushing a wheelchaired husband, my heart goes out to her because I know what herculean efforts have gone into this public presentation of normalcy; the washing, wiping, cleaning up urine and feces, dressing and feeding that was preparatory to this trip and are her twenty-four-hour responsibility. Few women who have undergone the wrenching experience of caring for a dying spouse will be eager to remarry and risk a repeat of this ordeal.

The high-rise buildings that line the main avenues of southern Florida are filled with white-haired widows who are active, involved and happy. They go to dances, which are very popular in Florida, designed to imitate the social functions of their youth and also to afford them chances to show off the mambo and samba lessons that cost them a small fortune. They go to meet men who they want to date and dance with but not marry.

"You see that guy sitting in the corner? He's not dancing because he just had a bypass. That one on the dance floor is OK now that he got his new pacemaker. They want to get married, I hear. A woman would be crazy to marry them, they're not looking for wives, they're looking for nurses!"

Men of that age and condition cannot live alone so they seek wives to cook for them, care for them and listen to their complaining which is a big part of such relationships. Menstrual cramps inure women to pain from an early age and they grow up with an almost stoic ability to deal with hurt and discomfort. My mother often had knife cuts on her fingers, ironing burn marks on her arms but I never heard her incur any of these bruises. My father, on the other hand, called the doctor when he caught his finger in a drawer. Men seem to be in constant need of sympathy and the more advanced in age they are, the more advanced their ailments and requisite demands for succor. Who needs it?

Most of these elderly widows have become savvy enough to realize the drawbacks of remarriage. Every widow I interviewed reiterated the relative contentment of living without the compromises required by a husband. Here are just some of the comments I heard:

"I have a wonderful busy life."

"I enjoy my privacy."

"I don't have to give in to anyone else, I do what I want."

"I can eat a grilled cheese at eleven o'clock if I feel like it and not have to shop and cook a big dinner."

"I found that there's life after men."

"What good are men, they don't have the same interests as women do, they never talk. Women always seem to dredge up something to talk about. You can sit at dinner with a man and not exchange a single word for an hour—unless you start up a conversation."

"I do fine handling my own life. I don't need any help."

"Who needs to wash another man's socks?"

"Who wants those old men? Do you know one date I had told me he couldn't get an erection and he wanted me to help? The nerve of him, I hardly knew the man and he wants me to go to bed with him and work yet."

Unfortunately, some widows get sucked into the old sales pitch that a woman needs a husband to take care of her, and that an unmarried woman is automatically banished into social exile. Bewildered by their new widowhood, afraid of the unknown, they are panicked into remarriage too quickly without allowing themselves the time to become acquainted with themselves and their abilities to live alone and like it.

The Dangers of a Rushed Remarriage

Debby's husband of forty-two years died after a long bout with cancer. She was weary, dispirited and grief-stricken. At sixty-seven years old she felt like eighty. Emerging from many years of being a wife, she had in essence lost her "job" and now perceived herself as being worthless. What would she do for the rest of her life?

A few months after her husband's death, she ran into Warren, an old friend who had moved away years earlier and had recently returned to the area. His wife had just died, also of cancer. Their common experience created a new empathy between them and they began to see each other regularly. After just three months, he asked her to marry him. She was stunned and totally unprepared. She had just about completed all the myriad of details and assorted legalities that ensue after death, like changing listings, redeeming insurance policies, and sundry assorted minutiae that must be handled by the surviving spouse. She had not yet had the time to start building a life on her own. She was uncomfortable, it all seemed too soon. Neither she nor Warren was concerned about the propriety of remarriage so shortly after their mates demises since the protracted dying period eliminated the need for extended mourning. But Debby was in a dilemma over how to respond to Warren's proposal.

Debby was uncertain and totally lacking in the confidence to make any major decisions. Her inadequacy made her the perfect prey of not-always-well-meaning friends and relatives who claim to know what's best for everyone. They pointed out what a great catch and once-in-a-lifetime opportunity this marriage offered ("You're not a youngster, you know. How many more chances will you get? If you don't grab him, there's a line of women who will. A good-looking well-to-do man like him can have his pick of younger women, you're lucky you caught him before he got out into the market").

Debby liked Warren, but did not love him. She found him pleasant and easy to be with. But perhaps practicality should outweigh passion at this time in life, right? Her husband just died, his wife just died, it seemed fortuitous . . . maybe even fated. So Debby said "yes."

The first stabs of disquiet came at the lawyer's office where they all met to sign the pre-nuptial agreements. Her children pointed out that their father's money should eventually rightfully be theirs and the only way to insure this was with an agreement. This seemed logical to Debby. The trouble came when she encountered the grasping hostility of Warren's three daughters who obviously regarded their father's new marriage as a plot to deprive them of their birthright. Warren tried to assuage their fears and after everybody had been fully assured by the attorneys that Debby's children would be her sole heirs and Warren's children would be his, the papers were signed. They quickly married and Debby moved into Warren's house since it was more luxurious and larger than hers.

It was strange for Debby to be living in another woman's house. She missed her small but familiar home which she had already rented to a French family who signed a two-year lease. Warren's house was nice, but it wasn't hers and when she expressed her discomfort, he insisted that she refurnish the house to suit her tastes.

The project started out as fun and Warren even joined her in the shopping. They started to enjoy selecting and discussing new pieces and color schemes. Then the daughters heard and came screaming.

"How dare you throw out my mother's furniture and drapes. It's all in perfectly good condition."

They accused Debby of senseless extravagance and told their father he had married a selfish woman who was trying to waste his money and should be controlled.

Debby was shocked. A rather shy, sensitive person, she did not know how to cope with such crude behavior and active hostility. She turned to Warren, expecting him to admonish his daughters for their insulting assault on his wife, and was stunned at his silence. He did not defend her, he did not explain that he had suggested the refurnishing, he did not chastise them for their reprehensible display of disrespect for an older woman. He did not warn them that attacks upon his wife would not be tolerated. He just sat there.

"What have I gotten into?" thought Debby in despair. "What kind of man is this? What kind of family is this that I am now part of?"

When she discussed his daughters' behavior with Warren after they had stormed out of the house, he was sheepish but not ashamed as Debby would have expected. In fact, he thought that she was overreacting because he assumed all mothers and daughters screamed at each other. He was surprised to hear that Debby's relationship with her daughter was calm and pleasant, and even though arguments occurred, insulting rudeness was unacceptable. He told her to disregard his daughters' behavior "They were just upset, they didn't mean half of what they said."

Those kind of battles were commonplace between his former wife and the girls and they all got over it in no time. Debby pointed out that whereas his wife was their mother, she was not, and emotional upheavals that take place between parents and children are totally different from those that occur with strangers.

"Oh, you're making too much of this, Debby," he said cajolingly. "Why don't we just forget the whole thing?"

But Debby could not, especially since his daughters made it their business to drop in constantly and made her feel that she was under active surveillance. They were sullen and ungracious and scanned the house constantly looking for additions or subtractions to the furnishings. There was an extremely unpleasant episode when one of the daughters spotted the unfamiliar silk bedspread in the master bedroom.

"How much did that fancy thing cost?" she demanded rudely. Debby looked at her quietly and answered,

"I really don't remember. I bought it six years ago."

The daughter did not apologize. Although Warren encouraged Debby to go ahead with her refurnishing plans, she lost heart and found the entire matter too distasteful. The prospect of having to defend her purchases to those harridans was not worth the acquisitions. Their constant remarks about the stupidity of buying new things when you're so old and the ridiculous amortization ratio of spending $1,000 for something that you'll barely live long enough to enjoy, were offensive and aggravating.

What was worse, however, was Warren's total inability to understand her resentment of his daughters' treatment of her.

"Just don't listen. Ignore them."

But she couldn't. Her whole life became polluted by the acrimony engendered by Warren's family. They resented her, they disliked her and they vented their feelings continually.

Warren was a nice man, and comparatively undemanding. She enjoyed his company and could have adjusted to serving dinners he liked, and arranging his clean laundry in his drawers the way he preferred. Having recently left one position as wife and housekeeper, it was simple to adapt to the new job. She was accustomed to serving and subordinating her wishes to those of a man. But she could not countenance the disruptive behavior of the daughters, nor what she considered her husband's lack of respect for her.

Then the day came when Warren announced that his daughters had convinced him to set up an Inter Vivos Trust whereby all his money would be put into a trust fund that they would manage. He explained that this was merely a device to avoid future inheritance taxes and would alter nothing in their present lives. When Debby mentioned this to her son who was a trust and estates attorney, he told her that Warren's ability to spend money would now be monitored by his children. She was horrified to realize that these hostile women would now have a say over whatever she bought and would in effect take control of her life. Her son noticed how upset she became and wanted to know why. Up to that point, she had never mentioned her unhappiness to her children feeling that this was her problem and she would handle it. As far as they knew, her marriage was fine. When her son heard the entire story that she poured out tearfully, he was infuriated. He wanted to confront Warren immediately but she pleaded with him to hold off until she had a chance to think things through and determine what action she wished to take.

The next morning over breakfast, Debby broached the subject with Warren and explained how difficult she would find living under the financial thumbs of his children. He became so upset that Debby feared he would make himself ill. She realized that although he presented a secure, masterful image, Warren was actually a weak, passive man who had always taken the path of least resistance which in this instance was to yield to his daughters' demands. Unlike most men who abhor scenes and are fiercely uncomfortable with overt female displays of emotion, Warren totally ignored them. He had grown up in a house full of women, his father died when Warren was a small child and he was brought up by his mother and grandmother. His married life was merely a continuation of a female household only this time it was a wife and daughters. Early on he had developed his own technique for living with women which consisted of being gentle, charming and helpless so that they adored him and turned themselves inside out to please him. He always walked away from their attacks, assiduously avoided confrontations, confident that their ire would pass and their long habit of looking after him would result in a happy ending. Debby was asking him to argue with his daughters, to take an assertive position that he never had assumed before. The concept was unthinkable.

Sorrowfully she realized that she could not change the habits of a lifetime, and that he would never fight for himself let alone for her. She knew that the only way her marriage would survive was to do what women have done for centuries—give in to her husband's needs. When she told her children of her decision to accept the terms of her marriage, they were upset. Especially her daughter.

"Mother, you have never even given yourself a chance to live alone and find out who you are and what you like. I saw you all my life doing for Dad, living the life he wanted and taking care of him. Now you're in another situation where again you're the caretaker and compromising to please a man. Leave him, and his horrible daughters. You don't need his financial support. Go back to your house and start a new life. Find out what it's like to please only yourself, to do whatever you want and not have to consider anyone else. Take the chance. You'll see, you'll love it."

Debby's son listened to his sister's impassioned plea, looked at his uncertain, frightened, close-to-tears mother, and said quietly: "But suppose she doesn't love it?"

Debby's eyes met her son's and she turned to her daughter and said: "No, I have to stay. I'll live with it."

She explained that the known difficulties she would now have to face were preferable to the unknown difficulties she would encounter in the totally unfamiliar life as a single woman. She had always lived this way and she was used to it. The idea of the terrible daughters doling out money was preferable to the fears she had of handling her own finances. Living with a man for whom she had lost all respect was still better than living with no man at all.

So she stayed, and faced the once-a-month criticism about her excessive number of long distance phone calls, questions about the need to have her hair and nails done every week, lifted eyebrows when she wore a new dress or pair of shoes. She hated the garish foil wallpaper in the bathroom and den, but knew that there was no possibility of alteration. And worst of all, she lived with a man who cared more for his own comfort and peace of mind than he did for her, whom she could never trust because in the last analysis, he was her husband but not her friend.

The Fear
of Financial Management

Debby was like a prisoner who is released after forty-two years and becomes a recidivist because of a now ingrained inability to cope with the complications and demands of freedom. All widows who have lived sheltered lives where the husbands took full charge of finances, billpaying, car maintenance and taking out the garbage, are frightened at first and the older they are, the more scared they are. At first, they recoil from the strange looking bills and statements which seem so forbidding. They marvel at the brilliance and capability of their husbands who were able to deal with all those complicated-looking papers. They become confused and angry and look for someone else, like a child or grandchild, to take charge of all these onerous details.

All they need is for someone to sit down with them, force them to confront the details, and show how easy it is to pay a bill and record payment, whether it be for a charge account, insurance premium, mortgage or rent. They start tentatively and then, surprised at the simplicity, get into more depth and eventually take tremendous pride in their ability to run their own affairs. You know they're OK when you hear:

"Huh, what's the big deal? Here I thought Sam was such a genius. Write a few checks, make a few notes, that's all there is to it."

My mother-in-law admired her husband extravagantly for what she thought was his intense business acumen because he had accounts in seven banks. After he died, and we were subjected to the nuisance of visiting seven banks to transfer funds, she realized that he kept a few thousand dollars in each merely to be able to boast every time they traveled through the city:

"You see that bank? We have money in there."

Her financial idol quickly developed clay feet, and in no time she was handling her own bills and banking. Once the money mystique, perpetuated by husbands who want to enslave wives into dependency, is exposed in all its actual simplicity, widows get down to the business of building lives of proud independence. When they finally have control of their own financial positions and futures—why should they even consider marrying again?

If Debby had not had the misfortune of being presented with an opportunity for remarriage so quickly after she became widowed, she would have been forced to face up to her imagined inadequacy. She would have gotten over the first fright of solitude, and learned to balance a checkbook, hire a contractor, buy her own car and deal with the details of running her own life. She could have developed a self-esteem that would never permit the kind of abuse she was now willing to accept from her husband and his family. But Debby was a victim of her time and was one of the unquestioning believers of the myth that a woman must marry in order to be a whole person. A definition of the word "myth" in *The American Heritage Dictionary of the English Language* states: "A notion based more on tradition or convenience than on fact." Just so—but whose convenience? Why, men's of course.

NINE

The
"Closet Singles"

I would be married,
but I'd have no wife
I would be married
to a single life.
> —RICHARD CRASHAW

THEY ARE ATTRACTIVE, charming women who were married briefly ten, twenty or thirty years ago and claim to want husbands but never seem to be able to find the right one. Of course not, because it's not men they find wanting—it's marriage.

How many times have you heard people say

"She was a young woman when she lost her husband. I wonder why she never married again?" Or "she's been divorced for ten years. She's a good looking woman—I wonder why she's still single?"

There is always the assumption that remarriage is every woman's goal and divergence from the pattern is puzzling. If she had never been married, well then she just wasn't the sort men find desirable but having proven her bride-ability there seems to be no rational reason why she hasn't found another husband. It's not because she has not been looking. Over the years she has gone out with a succession of men and continues to reiterate that she wants to get married. But as my father used to put it "She can't get anyone to take her to the altar."

Did it ever dawn on them, both the social commentators and the women themselves, that they do not WANT to get married ever again . . . that the one experience was disenchanting and once the terrible spinster taboo had been lifted they were able to relax into the pleasures of singlehood freedom?

Single
& Savoring It

These women are "closet singles" who have built highly satisfactory lives for themselves and are reluctant to rearrange their homes and activities and priorities to adapt to the needs of men. They did that already and it wasn't worth it. The truth is they do not want to be wives. Maybe they never did. They lead busy, fulfilling lives with the privileges of glorious freedom that married women often envy; they never have to cope with a man's demands, they never have to clean up another person's messes, they never have to deal with any neuroses and needs except their own, they never have to mold their mentalities to conform to the compromises required to live happily with husbands. They are single and they love it.

Unfortunately, society has not allowed them to admit this heretical fact either to the world at large or even to themselves. So they wear wedding bands to prove that someone wanted them once and continue to feel disquietingly different.

Worldly but "Wedded"

Madeline is now in her seventies and still wears the wedding band from a marriage that took place fifty years ago and lasted for two years before she divorced a husband who consummated the marriage on their wedding night and then gave up the disgusting habit at once. The lump sum settlement her lawyer wisely advised her to accept and invest has kept her comfortable all these years.

Madeline still lives in the house that she came to as a bride and has filled it with memorabilia of her life and elegant souvenirs of her travels. A woman of impeccable taste, she has furnished the house with the carefully chosen antiques accumulated with the eyes and skill of an expert which she has become. What began as an interest developed into a hobby and then a profession as Madeline discovered she had an innate artistry that led to her becoming a writer and lecturer on art and antiques. Every corner of her house shows the talents of the owner and is obviously lovingly cared for with pride and pleasure.

Everybody has tried to "fix her up" with someone. Over the years, she has had a succession of lovers and wild romantic affairs that were the despair and envy of her sister and friends.

"Why don't you pick someone marriageable for once?" they would cry as she trotted out another of the charming but elusive rogues who would do deliciously unpredictable things like carrying her off to the Riviera on a whim, or see to it that she had a roomful of roses when she arrived at a hotel on one of her many trips everywhere.

"He said he plans to divorce his wife," she would explain to everyone. "She doesn't understand him and he's very unhappy but there are the children . . ."

She was rarely without a man. There was always someone who was dancing attendance and even some who were allowed to move in, for a while. Like the charming Frenchman who was here to have an eye operation and wore a dashing eyepatch during his period of convalescence in her home. She was very skilled at attracting men, and adept at keeping them as long as she wanted. When the dashing Frenchman started to flirt with the wife of a couple who had been invited to drinks and dinner, the guests found themselves on the street after cocktails with the husband accusing his wife of misunderstanding the invitation.

Her dresser drawers were always filled with the sort of stunning salacious underwear and nightgowns that married women stare at in windows and wonder who wears them.

She continued to bemoan the marital unsuitability of all the men she seemed to meet, yet she never chose anyone who wasn't. She did not need financial support so fiscal standing was never a criterion. But stability and the desire to settle down were traits she should have sought if she really wanted to marry.

Madeline claimed that she loved children and wanted to be a mother. But her two nieces seemed to fulfill her maternal instinct yet not interfere seriously with her life. They adored her. She was so much more fun than their serious and disciplined mother and was always involved in interesting activities. They loved her, and gave her the comfort of knowing that someone would always be there when needed. Her sister provided the same security in Madeline's life and also the role of the stern disapproving guardian who watched over her best interests at all times.

Madeline was six years younger than her sister who she always regarded as their father's favorite. Like many siblings, each child had a totally different view of their family life. Her sister saw their upbringing as satisfactory, normal and happy, whereas Madeline remembered only a father who disapproved of her frivolity and disparaged her creativity. Her mother she saw as a sensitive and loving woman who suffered the bullying of an arrogant tyrannical husband. Both daughters dutifully married sons of approved families, but whereas her sister was content to live with a boring man in a totally predictable existence that replicated that of generations of women before her, Madeline wanted more.

A product of her time and upbringing, she would have stayed in the dull, restrictive marriage and never taken the revolutionary step of divorce had not her husband committed the sin that was abhorred by even the most conventional, traditional families—he failed to perform the basic male marital obligation of providing his wife with children and not because he was sterile but because he was sexually neuter. In her virginal innocence, Madeline had no way of knowing during the first year of her marriage that her husband's lack of ardor was unusual and the fact that he desired sexual intercourse only three times during the entire twelve months was not normal behavior for a twenty-five-year-old man. Then one Sunday they were in their parents' kitchen doing the dishes together after a family dinner and her sister asked why she was not yet pregnant. When Madeline mentioned her infrequency of procreational activity, her sister reacted with shock, and for the first time Madeline realized something was wrong. Her sister advised their parents immediately and Madeline's incensed father arranged a family meeting with the miscreant groom's parents who were totally unmoved and unimpressed by the accusation that their son was not properly performing his marital obligations. Their reaction plus the fact that they had but the one child made Madeline's father deduce that the sluggish sex drive may have been hereditary.

"I don't see what's so terrible," said the mother of the groom. "He's still a good husband and provider and at least she'll never have to worry about him running around with other women."

Although her father had always regarded divorce as unmentionable and unthinkable, he felt it was righteous and appropriate under the circumstances and arranged the entire matter. Together with a wise attorney, they saw to it that Madeline was well compensated for the indignity she had undergone. Her husband had despoiled and disappointed her and forced her into the ignominious role of divorcee, a shameful epithet in those days, and thus must pay her well for his misdeed.

Madeline usually rebelled against her father's orders but this time she accepted unhesitatingly and gratefully. In truth, she was relieved to be rid of the husband who she found totally uninspiring and a life she found stultifying.

She found herself in the pleasant position of being the pathetic wronged woman and was treated sympathetically and almost tenderly by her father for the first time in her life. Everyone felt sorry for her and wanted to help reestablish her life and, of course, find another husband. She was invited to endless dinner parties to meet eligible males and found herself enjoying a freedom and sense of abandon she had never experienced before. Since she was now a married woman, she was allowed to live in her own apartment and not reside with her parents as did all proper single girls. She had a lovely home all to herself with no oppressive father or husband to impose demands, and a frantically busy social life that had her out most nights of the week. She was pretty, she was intelligent, and she was FREE. She loved it, but still mindful of the conditioning that unmarried means unwanted, she wore the wedding ring that branded her Mrs. forever. And she embarked on a life that would have been totally satisfactory had she not been burdened with that emotional baggage of feeling that unmarried is unnatural.

Madeline knew plenty of married couples. By and large, she saw little she coveted. Though she professed to envy her sister's constant access to an escort and secure connubial life, she considered her brother-in-law a crashing bore and the idea of living with such a man to be a punishment. She regarded all the men she knew and had ever known as nice to visit but she wouldn't want to live with them.

Madeline is a "Closet Single." She never wanted to be married, but she cannot admit the fact even to herself. How much happier she would have been were she a product of now and not then. Even in a conservative country like England, young women today have become liberated to the point where current British books will contain passages like this that appeared in Michael Underwood's *Death at Deepwood Grange*:

"Rosa not infrequently despaired of her so-called love life, though not as often as her friends did. The young men who were trotted out for her approval usually left her cold and the few short-lived affairs she had had were always with impudently amoral young men who would make hopeless husbands and fathers, whatever their attractions in bed. Even so, she regarded herself as more fulfilled than a lot of her married girlfriends who took it upon themselves to despair in her behalf."

Today it is easier for women to decide to not marry because they have more resources and recourses. Years ago, the "single-minded" woman who was conventional and not courageous plowed ahead into miserable matrimony and was only freed by fate.

Divorce:
The Freedom Factor

Betty was a spunky bubbly redhead of nineteen when she caught the eye of a thirty-two-year-old bookstore owner in her town who fell madly in love with her and proposed within one month after their meeting. The year was 1935 and in those days an offer of marriage from a respectable, responsible businessman was considered a coup for any young girl. Betty was infatuated with John and her friends thought she was the luckiest girl in the world because he was so intelligent and nice-looking even though his hair was starting to thin a bit on top. And she wouldn't have to live in a one-room apartment with a young callow husband who was not yet established, and maybe even work to help pay the bills until he could make enough to support the household. John had a large sunny five-room apartment over the store and it was rumored that he owned the building, for gosh sakes. They could even afford to have a baby right away if she wanted instead of having to wait a few years until they had built up a bank account. Of course, Betty's parents approved heartily of the match and considered themselves fortunate that this serious prosperous man would take charge of their very attractive daughter whose popularity with the boys had always caused problems of discipline and control at home. The wedding was an elaborate affair after which they honeymooned in Bermuda and returned to settle into a life of domesticity and, Betty assumed, automatic bliss.

At first, it was a novelty. But soon Betty began to miss everything and everyone. Married life involved a good deal of drudgery and not too much fun. Betty was a gregarious, energetic woman who enjoyed exploring new situations and new people. John preferred to sit quietly and read on the few evenings he was home since the store kept him busy six days and three nights a week. Like women of that era, Betty adjusted her preferences to suit his and they lived a sedate and uneventful existence.

Once the awe of her husband subsided, Betty began to realize that they had little in common and in fact, she found him unexciting and unappealing. She mentioned her discontent to her mother, who assured her that she would feel differently if she became pregnant because having a child keeps a woman busy and fulfilled.

They had a son the following year and Betty became even more unhappy. She loved the baby and was a good mother, but caring for an infant involved twenty-four hours of slavery which left her exhausted. Fatigue gave her a good reason to refuse the sexual demands of her husband which she found tiresome and totally unsatisfying and made her wonder what was the big deal people made about sex. Since she had to be up at night with the baby and John needed his rest in order to be alert the next day for work, Betty convinced him that for the time being, it would be best if he slept in the spare bedroom while she kept the infant in the room with her.

By the time the baby was a year old, their life had solidified into separate bedrooms and neither made an effort to change the arrangements, which was fine with Betty. John's business had grown and there were now three stores which kept him away almost every evening and often weeks at a time when he had to make buying trips or attend conventions.

Six years passed and their son was in school, leaving Betty somewhat free for the first time in years. She began taking courses to resume the education she had abandoned when she married. She loved the work, she loved the interaction with other students, she loved just getting out of the house and doing something of value. Then one day, needing stamps to mail off a school paper to her professor, and knowing that her husband kept some in his briefcase, she opened the case and found stamps, but also photographs of John and a woman in various stages of nudity. Her initial reaction was shock and anger. Her second thought was to hire a detective who followed her husband long enough to catch him and the other woman in bed in a hotel room thereby supplying the legal evidence required in that state for a divorce.

Armed with alimony from a guilty spouse, Betty moved to the big city, placed her son in a good boarding school and for the first time in her life found herself totally free. She got her degree and then became executive secretary to the head of a vast international charity organization. In the 1980's, a woman like Betty would have started in an executive position but in the 1940's you began at the typewriter and worked your way up, which she did. Today she is the head of a large organization, travels all over the world and has just broken up with her latest lover.

During the interim years, she had many dates and relationships always with the stated intention that she wanted to find a good husband. Yet when a man's interest became too intense and the possibility of marriage became imminent, Betty found a reason to cut things off. Everyone wanted to match her up with some man or other, but it never seemed to work out.

"I can't understand it," friends continued to comment. "She's so pretty, and has such a marvelous personality, you'd think she'd find a husband in a minute."

She would have—if she wanted one. But deep down, Betty rejects marriage because she prefers to live her own life alone. Her son is now grown, married and lives in another state and they have a fine relationship. She has everything she wants when and where she wants it—so why should she marry? She tried it and found she likes single better. Now if she could only admit this to her friends and to herself, she would be happily free of that burden of guilt borne by all women who feel that they are in some way inferior if they do not have proof of ownership of a man—marriage.

The "Looking for Mr. Perfect" Excuse

She's attractive, she has lovers and talks constantly of her desire to marry—when the right man comes along. That's a never-married "closet single."

Roberta, the pretty, well-groomed fortyish grade school teacher I interviewed for this book immediately announced that she was not a suitable subject since she has always wanted to get married.

"Then why didn't you?" I asked.

Her face registered surprise mixed with pleasure. It was probably the first time in twenty years that anyone had made the assumption that her single state was due to her choice. She proceeded to prove my point by regaling me with "horror" stories of the dozens of flawed men she has had the misfortune to encounter since puberty. Each one had some disgusting drawback or character defect that soon became apparent as their friendship developed. No matter how great a man looked at the inception of their relationship, her glorious expectations of perfection were inevitably shattered as familiarity lowered the behavior barriers and he proved himself to be merely human and therefore unacceptable. She assured me each time she met a new man, she embarked on the friendship with an open heart and mind, filled with the romantic expectation that here at last was the husband of her dreams who would treat her with adoration and consideration and make her "feel good about herself" (a modern term of nauseating narcissism). And each time she had to suffer her mother's constant "so when?" phone calls replete with discussions about the potential wedding guest list.

But alas, when the courtship period passed and the relationship evolved into normal give and take, Roberta became disenchanted and refused to take what she saw as the little he was able to give thereby proving himself to be another man unworthy of the position as her husband.

When I asked for specific examples of ways in which this succession of swains had failed, she cited a litany of complaints similar to those heard at every ladies' luncheon table where the prime topic is usually husband-bashing. "He never talks, he never listens, he never appreciates, he forgets, he never understands." (Have you ever noticed that whereas men criticize what women do, women criticize what men do *not* do?)

What she, and other "closet singles" view as unforgivable and unendurable are irritants, annoyances and manifestations of male weaknesses that married women are willing to accept because they obviously find the quid pro quo worth the compromise.

Why should she have to compromise if she prefers a free life unfettered by connubial demands? Instead of facing the fact that she truly does not want to marry, she persists in the search for The Perfect Man laying out a job description that sounds like a composite of Sir Lancelot, Robert Redford and Lee Iacocca.

This woman cannot simply relax and enjoy the pleasures of her chosen single life. Instead, she tortures herself with the eternal quest. To reach for the unreachable star may be fine for the Man of La Mancha, but it's a drag for the woman of today. She could be comfortable and happy with her lifestyle if she did not pollute her pleasure with a sense of failure that makes her feel unworthy and unwanted and ultimately destroys the possibility of her ever having a happy male-female relationship, married or unmarried.

The "closet single" woman frequently has a perennial "boyfriend," a man who has been hanging around like a puppy for years and would marry her like a shot but whose attentions she alternately scorns, takes advantage of, and takes for granted. Like Groucho Marx who stated that he would never want to join any club that would find him acceptable, this man's very availability makes him unappealing and knocks him out of the running for the role of Her Husband.

There will never be a Mr. Right because she doesn't want to be Mrs. Right but doesn't have the courage to face that fact and her mother. She is a "closet single" and will only be happy when she stops listening to any voices other than her own.

"Closet singles" perpetuate their own misery by their inability and/or unwillingness to confront the realization that, for whatever reasons, they truly do *not* want to be married. Frequently conventional women, they shrink at admitting to heterodoxy which would brand them with the dread word "different." They whine about the injustice of Fate that has deprived them of a husband and continue to pursue a lifestyle that precludes all possibilities of acquiring one.

The Marriage-Prevention Lifestyle

"How did I get to be forty and not married?" Cora cried last year. A self-supporting computer operator, she had been contentedly living with Ralph for fifteen years when suddenly she decided she should get married because everyone else seemed to be. Their life together quickly deteriorated into anger, accusations and decisions to leave him, then stay with him and an up and down existence that began to drive both of them crazy.

When they met, Cora was a pretty, happy twenty-five-year old with vague ideas of settling down someday but not quite yet. Ralph was a free spirit type who made his living refinishing furniture, punctuated with winter trips to the Caribbean and the Florida Keys where he worked for scuba diving schools. He was romantic and adoring and she loved him and/or the life (she was never sure which). Cora quit her job and traveled with Ralph picking up work wherever they stopped for the winter. They never mentioned marriage because the concept of home and family never entered the picture. As the years went on, they decided to settle in one place and rented a small house in the suburbs where he opened his own refinishing business and she became a Kelly Girl part-time computer operator. When she hit forty, Cora began to think she ought to have a home and children but with whom? She had never viewed Ralph as a husband and father. He was just the man she ate with, had sex with and shared a house with but he did not fit the image she had of The Protector Man of the House like her father.

She began to observe married couples looking for signs of closeness, caring and respect that she had never built into her relationship with Ralph because they both wanted an independence and individuality that discouraged the collaborative efforts required of marriage. Every aspect of Cora's life was constructed to carefully avoid responsibility of any kind. She would not take a full-time job although she could earn double what she did as a temp and have the security of medical and pension benefits. Her refusal was not based on laziness or fear of work; there were many weeks when she put in weekends and nine and ten hours a day. Rather she needed to know that she could be free whenever she chose and preferred to work on her own terms.

Which is just how she wanted everything . . . on her own terms.

Now suddenly she wanted the American

dream—the whole enchilada . . . husband, house, kids. Most people seem to be married and happy. Her sister and brother were married, why wasn't she? Their conventional lives which she had always viewed as banal and dreary now became the ideal state of being. Cora began to re-evaluate Ralph, no longer seeing him as the pleasant man she liked coming home to, but as an infuriatingly unaffiliated guy who acted nothing like the husbands she had met. She wanted a baby, but how could she possibly consider unreliable Ralph as a father?

Ralph found himself living with a carping nag who demanded attention, visible displays of affection, manifestations of caring and constant revelation of his feelings about her, his work and the world. He was puzzled and confused, and hated to see her so unhappy. Every other day there was some confrontation about his failure to perform as Cora now wanted.

"We don't communicate!" she would shriek. "Talk to me, for God's sakes!" Mystified and miserable, Ralph was unable to please her. They lived by rules of privacy and independence that had been mutually established years ago but were now apparently unacceptable to Cora.

"Do you want to get married?" he continued to ask and she continued to refuse because she had an idealized image of marriage that was as flesh-and-blood as the bride and groom on a wedding cake. There was no way Ralph (or any man) could fit the picture. In reality, their relationship was a good one and in many ways undistinguishable from many perfectly successful marriages. But that was not the issue.

If Cora truly wanted to be a wife and mother, she would have either married Ralph or moved out and sought a new relationship. But she did neither because she did not want to give up the freedom of being single which allowed her to do whatever she wanted and to take off whenever she wanted.

She really enjoyed her life with Ralph and their living arrangements had always pleased her enormously. Until she reached forty and the old spinster conditioning hit her like a ton of bricks. Then she wanted a quick role change without any of the obligations that went with the job. Cora had eschewed marriage because it did not suit her needs and nature, yet she cannot cope with the cliche image her single state conveys. Like most "closet singles," she is torn between the desire to conform and the need to be different. So she tortures herself with the usual "closet single" self-flagellation behavior of setting up impossible standards for a marriage partner and then agonizing over her inability to find him.

It takes a tremendous amount of self-awareness and courage to kick over cultural stereotypes set down by society and your mother. But as more and more young women are doing it, older women should be encouraged to be single if they choose.

No woman should ever feel she has to conceal her wish to *not* marry, from herself or anyone else. Nor should she be made to feel guilty because she has chosen to take a life route that has not been prescribed as regular and average. We live in a wonderfully free era when everyone is coming out of the closet and all sorts of behavior and lifestyles are being accepted, condoned and even commended. Being unmarried is not unnatural—if it works for you it's wonderful.

The Myth of Maiden Aunts: More to Be Praised Than Pitied

Freedom is a system based on courage.
—CHARLES PEGUY

"LET'S ASK poor Aunt Martha to Christmas. She must be so lonely."

So the pathetic maiden aunt arrives in her new car wearing designer clothes and a mink bearing armloads of gifts for her great nieces and nephews, has a wonderful time and goes home to her quiet and elegantly furnished highrise apartment leaving her harried niece to put five screaming children to bed and straighten up the mess in her cramped split level living room after which she falls into an exhausted sleep ready to be up at six-thirty to prepare breakfast for seven people, make the beds, clean the bathrooms and start thinking about lunch.

Who's to be pitied here?

The unmarried older woman has always been regarded as a sad figure whom we view sympathetically with just a touch of condescension. After all, she's a reject doomed to live outside of the normal mainstream of family life. She'll always be an invited guest, an appendage but never really an integral part of the proceedings. Of course, she had her chances (a favorite family allegation to mitigate the premise that this female relative is not a total disaster) but she never had what it takes to persuade any man to choose her for his wife. Such a pity, she would have made a wonderful mother and helpmeet.

The presumption is always that the unmarried woman was unwanted and would certainly have chosen matrimony if only given the opportunity.

Contrast this dismal portrait with that of bachelor Uncle Bill, the same age as Martha, and doesn't he cut a dashing figure? Why Bill could charm the birds out of the trees. He's out with a different woman every night, he plays the field does jaunty Bill. He'll never marry; why should he buy a cow when milk is so cheap? He buys a new car every two years, wears expensive clothes, has a great bachelor pad, is welcomed at every family celebration and regarded with admiration tinged with envy.

Roget's *Thesaurus*'s synonyms for unmarried man are bachelor and misogynist, meaning one who hates women indicating a fellow who has deliberately avoided tying himself up with the disliked species. There is no such parallel synonym for an unmarried woman. All she can be called is spinster or old maid; there is no word to indicate her state could in any way be connected to choice.

But wasn't it? Isn't it time we looked back and started to reevaluate the position and motivations of maiden aunts and spinsters who have been so mistreated and misread? Substitute the name Martha for Bill in the above profiles and it would play just as well. Perhaps all those maiden aunts and spinster schoolteachers we and our mothers remember from childhood were more to be praised than pitied. Conceivably they viewed marriage and all its concomitant benefits and drawbacks and decided that the negatives outweighed the positives and made the calculated courageously non-conformist choice to NOT marry.

In the 1920's and thirties, the school systems were filled with spinster schoolteachers who were regarded as forbidding but pathetic. Every respectful and slightly scared pupil's mother who was summoned before them could relieve her tension by feeling smug because after all, she had a husband and children while this pitiful woman could not even get herself a man. Let's review the realities of that era and see who was the one to be pitied.

The Single
Escape from Drudgery

Ethel was the fifth of eleven children living in a crowded two-bedroom apartment with one bathroom. Her parents were Irish immigrants who slept on a couch in the living room while the children doubled and tripled up in the bedrooms. Ethel was a good student and somehow always managed to find a corner in which to do her homework. Although her mother barely had time to glance at her report card when she signed it, Ethel agonized over any mark below A. She adored and admired her teachers and was secretly determined to become one.

As she grew up, she saw her older sisters marrying and having babies immediately. She went out with boys, but school was her major interest and the family laughingly called her "the little bookworm." Unlike some of her elder siblings, Ethel finished high school and then announced to everyone's shock that she was going on to college. There were many free tuition schools available in the area to young women who had the marks to qualify, and Ethel did. Because her financial contribution to the family was needed, she worked evenings and weekends all through college.

Her sisters and mother could not understand Ethel. "You're going to get married and have kids anyway so why do you want to go to college? Go to secretarial school, get a nice office job so you can make good money until you get married. College is a waste of time for girls." But it was her time and her decision.

After college, Ethel got a job as an elementary school teacher in another neighborhood and shocked her family by announcing that she was moving into her own apartment. In those days, young ladies lived at home with their parents until marriage and continued to contribute to the financial maintenance of the household. Decent women did not live alone, it was unseemly. Ethel hated to make her parents unhappy, and she used as her main argument that she would need room to mark papers and do lesson preparation. Where would she do it in the crowded apartment with all those noisy younger brothers and sisters running about? She was finally able to get her parents' consent when she found an apartment in a Woman's Residence which conveyed the cachet of respectability her family could accept.

Ethel moved into the apartment and was absolutely ecstatic. For the first time in her life she had her own space, privacy and her own bathroom. She wallowed in the joys of furnishing it to her own taste. She loved the pleasure of eating alone, doing what she wanted and when she wanted. She went out to dinner and theatre with friends and developed an active social life. There were boyfriends who took her dancing, to the movies and sometimes on full-day outings which were fun. She loved her work, she enjoyed her independence, and ability to indulge herself and buy luxuries. It was heady stuff, and her mother's continual reminders that she was getting on in years and had better find a husband fast were falling on her progressively deafer ears.

Ethel went to family functions and saw her sisters' lives of virtual slavery as they cooked, cleaned, and cared for a growing stream of children. She enjoyed the hectic get-togethers and sharing the love and affection of the burgeoning brood, but she was glad to get home to her peaceful enclave and back to her very satisfying life. Then her boyfriend asked her to marry him. Ethel was surprised by her own reaction. Every young woman is primed for the joy of the big moment when she gets her proposal of marriage, it is the culmination of every little girl's dreams and the time when she can run to her mother and say proudly:

"I did it!"

Yet Ethel felt no exhilaration, but instead was troubled. She pleaded for time to give him her answer, and did not mention his proposal to her mother because she knew that the family would pressure her to say "yes." Indeed, they would regard her as a lunatic if she said anything else. He had talked about wanting to take care of her and protect her, and she thought: "Protect me from what?" The days of dragons are over and she was coping with life's vicissitudes extremely well all by herself. "Take care of her?" Didn't that actually mean have her take care of him, run his household, do his laundry? She did not need him for support, in fact, she had a better income, job and financial security than he did. So what beneficial life change was he offering? She saw the drudgery that women were committed to in marriage and contrasted it to her own lovely orderly existence. Of what would she be deprived if she said "no"? True she would probably not see him anymore but although she liked him very much, it was not an overpowering passion and she could live without him. If she chose to eschew marriage altogether, she would be giving up motherhood. But she had grown up in a large family and already had twenty-three nieces and nephews. True, they were not her children but then they were also not her responsibility.

Ethel thanked him very much but said "no" as she did to the few subsequent proposals received from other suitors. As the years passed, she travelled every summer and saw every part of the world. She moved ahead in her career and became the principal of her school, a position she thoroughly enjoyed. Her excellent performance drew national attention and she was invited to the White House for educational symposiums. But at Christmas, she always managed to spend the holidays with some of her nieces and nephews.

"Of course we'll ask your poor Aunt Ethel. After all, the sad little thing has no family of her own."

* * *

It is time for a revisionist view of the history of maiden aunts and spinsters, these much maligned women who have been portrayed in literature as sad creatures who are slightly dotty and usually eccentric bordering on imbecility. Even Miss Jane Marples, Agatha Christie's famed maiden sleuth, although exhibiting the brains to solve thorny mysteries is portrayed as a provincial "pussy" as the English refer to an unmarried lady of advanced years and slightly diminished capacity.

The presupposition that all such women were left unmarried because no men found them desirable is ludicrous. How many of these women made value judgments about the benefits of marriage and merely decided against it—and *chose* to take no husband? Given the subordinate position of wives years ago, both socially and legally, their choice was intelligent and courageous. They risked ridicule, being the butt of barbs of crude men who treated them with condescension and said behind their backs, "All she really needs is a good . . ." They risked being viewed as socially crippled because they are assumed to be virgins who are terminally deprived of the transcendent experience of sexual intercourse and, therefore, according to Dr. Freud, destined to go through life embittered and frustrated. They risked being regarded in many ways as second-class citizens of the world . . . and yet they made the choice. To opt to remain unmarried then in a world of marrieds took the kind of guts and strength of character that should forever erase the epithets of timid, pathetic and pitiful as applied to maiden aunts.

ELEVEN

Be a Smart Single; The Legal and Financial Ways to Protect Your Future

All's love, yet all's law.
—ROBERT BROWNING

IT'S GREAT to be your own boss, responsible to no one but yourself, which is probably one of the reasons you elected to be single. This means, however, that you alone are responsible for yourself and should set up a financial plan that will provide for

195

your future. Remember that the sole income stream into the household comes from you and you must prepare for the time when that flow ceases. This involves planning and learning about your rights as a single person and some of the wrongs that you can right in advance.

Unfortunately, the discipline required to plan and think ahead is often antithetical to the devil-may-care attitude of single people who tend to live for today and the hell with tomorrow. Being a woman carries the additional burden of the inculcated belief that legal and financial matters are a man's province and girls don't have that sort of capability. All this leads to a tendency to procrastination and relegating the job of working out financial plans to the category of defrosting the refrigerator and cleaning out closets. Let me point out the difference: this chore, which involves just a small investment of time can have a large effect on your future. Once you have completed the basic plan, you only have to review it from time to time to bring the figures up to date. So get yourself in hand and do it . . . now.

There is a special fiscal handicap to being single: the very freedom from restraints you so enjoy can lead to a profligacy and self-indulgent spending that can be dangerous. When there's no husband to curtail your whims ("A hundred bucks for a pair of brown shoes? What the hell for? You already have brown shoes"), your tendency may be to buy whatever strikes your fancy. The carping of a budget-minded spouse may be a drag but it can also serve to put the brakes on the kind of impulse buying that put big dents in the exchequer. Single living is devoted to total self-gratification, which makes the present a delight but can put the future in jeopardy. It's fun to hop a flight to Barbados when the slushy winter gets you down. It's tempting to buy the CD player you've been longing for when you see it on sale. Why shouldn't you spend money freely, it's your money and there's no one to worry about but you. Exactly. And there's no one to take care of you but you. Which is why it is so important for a single person to plan and prepare for her future.

If you are a single parent, you not only have to worry about yourself but your children as well and you must provide for their well-being, education and inheritance.

According to Michael J. Mella, a Certified Financial Planner with the Turcan Financial Group, Inc., of Rye, New York, there are specific procedures a single person should follow in order to insure a secure future.

Budgeting

The first step involves that painful self-analysis of spending called "Making a Budget." The very sound is a downer but it is imperative to know exactly how you stand and how much you need every month to maintain yourself in the style to which you have become accustomed. This requires your setting aside one evening, or Sunday morning, to address yourself to the realities of your cash flow, how much comes in each month and how much goes out. Sit down at a table with a large pad, pencil and all last year's bills and check stubs, a supply of Snickers and Twinkies to help your morale through this torturous exercise, and then put on your phone answering machine so you won't have any excuse to be lured away from this distasteful task.

Start the list with FIXED EXPENSES (OVERHEAD) like rent, or co-op maintenance, mortgage payments if you own a house or apartment, utilities (don't fool yourself that the phone bill was so astronomical last month only because of that guy you met from Colorado, chances are it's close to that figure every month), car payments, insurance.

Then start another heading: CLOTHING and another TRAVEL AND ENTERTAINMENT. This is when you are forced to face the horrific facts of credit card life. Set up columns for groceries, commutation to and from work, and one called MISCELLANEOUS that covers everything with no known category (such as those impulse items like cassettes, VCR tapes and that antique Persian rug you couldn't resist). Total all the lists to get a handle on expenses. On the other side list your total annual income, and hope that the income was greater than the outgo. But be prepared to face "stock taking shock," which is why the Snickers and Twinkies are kept handy. You may be stunned to find out how much you fritter away and how much higher your overhead is than you believed which would account for the puny condition of your savings account.

The newly widowed or divorced woman will

find tremendous benefit from this exercise. If her married arrangement had been to leave all financial matters to her husband, then this will be an invaluable introduction to the realities of handling money. The divorced woman will have to deal with the undoubtedly radical change in her assets, liabilities and income.

OK, the worst part is over. You have now accumulated all the facts you need to go ahead. Now it's time to *plan* for your near and distant future.

Saving

The first chore is to go over all lists other than FIXED EXPENSES (OVERHEAD) and start to cut. See how much of the unnecessaries and frivolities can be redirected into a solid savings and investment plan. Set a figure that you know you must put away each week or month and in that way impose a discipline that will become a way of life. Even if it's twenty dollars a week, once you develop the habit of banking it regularly you can then aim to save at least ten percent of your gross income.

This enables you to build up the all-important Emergency Fund that is absolutely necessary for every single person. It is, in effect, a cash cushion (note the word "cash") to get you over any hump and through any unexpected disaster. For instance, suppose you lose or leave your job, how will you cover expenses during the no-income period? Or you own a house and the furnace needs replacement or the water heater dies. According to Mike Mella, this Emergency Fund must be instant cash, like treasury bills or money market or bank account so that you can get your hands on it instantly. Mutual Funds or stocks may be easily converted into needed cash, but selling them at the wrong time could incur a large loss. It is suggested that this Emergency Fund consist of three to six months' living expenses.

Insurance

What about the possibility of you becoming sick or disabled? This is where INSURANCE comes in, especially Disability Insurance because who will support you if you cannot work?

"Income taxes and long-term disability," says Mella, "are the greatest obstacles to wealth accumulation for single individuals."

If you were to become disabled for a long time, and there's no second income to get you through, you could be wiped out. Suppose you fell and broke an arm or a leg or both and were unable to work for many months. Your employer would probably pay you for a specified period of time but then you would be on your own. Even if your company provides disability coverage, a group plan may well be insufficient. Usually it returns no more than 60 percent of your salary, and then there's a thirty- to ninety-day waiting period, and the benefit payout period may stop well short of sixty-five. Furthermore, you may not be covered for partial disability.

A number of insurance companies offer individual disability plans that can be used to supplement a group plan, or provide a full plan if you are self-employed. Discuss it with your insurance agent, describe your needs and financial position, and ask for his advice. When I bought my disability insurance policy some years ago, my agent recommended one company because they paid claims promptly, without major hassling. He was right. That's the kind of experience and knowledge that helps you make the correct decision. However, you have to ask questions and read the fine print. For instance, what is the policy's definition of disability? As reported in *U.S. News & World Report*'s August 3, 1987, cover story "Living Alone," shopping for disability insurance means reading the policies carefully to find the one that offers terms suitable to your particular work situation. Suppose your career involves two income-producing occupations, could you be denied benefits because only one of your two occupations is hampered by your disability? The example given by Dan McGill, head of the insurance department at the Wharton School warns "A concert pianist who loses a finger could collect under an 'own occupation' plan even if he were to teach." In other words, his disability has prevented him from pursuing his principal occupation. If he had a clause called "any occupation," which meant he could make money another way, he would not be able to collect. That's why a good tip is to talk to the insurance agent from whom you bought

201

the policy before you file a disability claim. Sometimes you inadvertently use the wrong words that might prejudice your case. Rely upon his experience to tell you exactly how you should describe the situation on the claim form.

Next we come to the other important insurance for singles, HEALTH AND MEDICAL INSURANCE. Check over the benefits your existing insurance offers. It is possible that the policy supplied by the company for which you work does not provide adequate coverage. We all have heard horror stories of people who thought their policies provided for specific contingencies and then when they were in the hospital learned that they were not covered or that there were cutoff limitations that left them with huge debts. There are all sorts of policies that cover you up to one million dollars and function as major medical supplements to your basic Blue Cross. These offer a diversity of benefits but if you do not read past the glowing promise headline atop the policy, you may be living under a dangerous misapprehension.

According to Carol R. Blucher, medical insurance specialist in Mamaroneck, New York, who counsels clients on how to select and collect health insurance, "It is important to analyze what the policy offers and see if the promised benefits coincide with your specific needs. For instance, as a person who lives alone, it is vital that your policy have a provision for home nursing care. Should you have an operation, or major illness, you will need some form of assistance at home until you are on your feet. Does your current policy offer this service? Read very carefully because insurance company terminology is imprecise to the point of misleading. They very often specify how many home health care visits you are entitled to for an entire year, and although the number sounds like a lot, ask how many hours constitutes one home visit. When you total up the true number of hours of nursing care they cover, it may not be sufficient should you need round-the-clock nursing for any length of time. Also note the specifics of who they designate can perform these services: must it be an RN or LPN, which means you cannot use your friendly neighbor or usual household help."

If you are recently widowed or divorced, employers must now let widowed and divorced spouses of medical group plan members continue coverage for up to three years as long as they pay the premiums themselves. Meanwhile, since individual policies can cost a fortune, check around to see if you belong to organizations or professional groups that offer members group coverage. Many religious organizations, churches and synagogues offer a wide range of major medical coverage. If you are over fifty, try AARP (American Association of Retired Persons), which has hospital and secondary range coverage policies that are excellent.

If you are self-employed or operate your own small business, check into organizations such as the Small Business Service Bureau, Inc., of Worcester, Massachusetts, who offer the bargains of group-purchased insurance to the small entrepreneur.

Do you need LIFE INSURANCE? Not if you are a single person. Of course, if you have children, then such coverage is important.

Buying a House or Apartment

One of the areas where single people are singled out unfavorably is the U.S. taxation system. The best tax shelter available to single people is actually home ownership. What other appreciated investment can be sold and the profits reinvested without having to pay income tax on the profits? And of course there are those lovely tax deductions for mortgage interest and real estate taxes.

Not so long ago, single women found it difficult to buy homes because they were considered risky prospects for mortgages. Women taking any kinds of loans were usually asked to have someone else co-sign. "We'll have to have your husband's name on the application, madame" was the usual response to any woman's request for bank money. Then the Fair Housing Act of 1968 and the Equal Credit Opportunity Act of 1974 made it illegal for lenders to deny a loan because of gender or marital status. Today, banks no longer look upon a female as the helpless hopelessly inept "little woman" but evaluate her as a loan prospect from the point of view of total income, stability of employment and credit history, just like real people. In 1985, 18 percent of all homes and 48 percent of condominiums were bought by singles, a good number of them women.

Real estate has proven to be a relatively safe and extremely profitable investment. Houses and apartments have doubled and tripled in value in the last ten years and have continued to increase. However, that does not necessarily mean that you should plunge into home buying without evaluating the benefits vs. drawbacks. It still may be better for you to rent.

Tally the costs of buying and owning—mortgage, taxes, insurance, maintenance, utilities—and offset the total by the tax benefits. Compare this total with the costs of renting, allowing for increases during the next few years. On the plus side of rental, add the interest you might be earning on the down payment. Then see if the concept of buying property rather than renting is right for you. Don't overlook the emotional factors, however, which are important in any major financial decision-making process. Do you feel that property ownership will give you a sense of solidity and belonging? Or would you find home maintenance responsibilities a heavy burden and would prefer to call the building management when the sink gets stuffed or the fridge breaks down?

Don't be swayed by the seductive lure of buying now and making a killing when you sell in the future, because the size of the profit is often determined by how far in the future you plan to move. When you sell, your property has to have appreciated enough so that you recoup not only the purchase price but the high cost of selling, the 1 to 3 percent in points to the lender, attorney's fees, title-search fees (required even if you bought the house just last month), and the roughly 6 percent broker's fee, which could be higher in your area. If you are in a career situation that requires transfers and the need to be able to pick up and move quickly, you can actually lose money on a house. The real estate market has been generally up, but in certain cities like Houston, for instance, you can find that the house you picked up at what you thought was such a bargain last year is worth half as much today, and you may not be able to find a buyer even at that depressed price.

If you have evaluated all the factors and decide to buy a house or apartment, figure out how much you can afford. Go to your bank, lay out your financial position for them and ask them to advise what price house you could carry. Lenders usually use two ratios as guidelines to calculate what they will lend: Your monthly mortgage payment (taxes and insurance cannot exceed 28 percent of your gross monthly income) and all debt payments should eat up no more than 36 percent. As far as the down payment is concerned, it ranges from 5 to 25 percent of the purchase price, depending on the lending institutions in your area, and the time you apply.

When you have found a house or apartment you like, make a bid that could be 15 to 25 percent less than the asking price. Don't be afraid to make a low offer; it's just the beginning of the negotiation. Once the seller accepts, be sure your contract gives you an out in the event of certain very real possibilities: Your engineer's inspection (which is an absolute necessity before buying) turns up some major construction flaws, or termite damage. Or your mortgage commitment falls through or a sudden rise in rates makes the whole deal unaffordable. If tenants live in the house, your lawyer's review of the lease indicates it may be tricky to get them out and you may have to incur heavy eviction costs, and long delays before you can actually take possession. Your lawyer, if he or she is experienced in real estate, will probably guide you in these areas, and put in the clause that the property be delivered broom clean and as promised giving you the right of 24-hours-before-closing inspection to ascertain that they haven't taken off with some of the fixtures that were to be included in the sale. If that happens, and let's say some of what looked like good appliances are either not working, or there at all, you may be able to knock down the price at closing.

Special Care for Special Situations

Not all singles are alike. There are variations that create the need for specific financial protection plans.

Single Mothers

You must carry adequate life insurance to provide for the support and education of your children and should begin a program of investing for their education right now.

Also check into your disability insurance and be sure the monthly payments are high enough to cover child care should you become incapacitated. You'll need someone to run the household and oversee the children if you are confined to bed. And be certain that your health insurance covers the children as well.

Divorced With Children

How much is the father providing for the children and how much will be your responsibility? When analyzing future needs and planning for children's education and support, the father's contribution will affect your budget and figures.

Like a single mother, you must examine your disability insurance and be sure payments are adequate enough to cover child care. Or can you depend upon the father to take the children for the period during which you are incapacitated? Are the children covered under their father's health insurance policies, or will this be your responsibility?

Widows

Assuming you have just received a chunk of money from insurance, you now have to protect that money from tax bites and work out an investment program that meets your needs. This requires the services of an accountant, lawyer or financial planner who will help you to minimize estate and income tax payments and could also advise you about investing.

Your income flow will now be different, of course, since you will be totally supported by your own earnings, if you work, plus monies generated from investments. It is vital for you to go through the budgeting analysis described above because you must become familiar with finances since you alone now have the responsibility. Remember that while it is helpful to get advice from financial experts, the decisions must be made by you and that requires knowledge.

When you are going over your budget and insurance costs, and you notice quarterly premiums for life insurance policies for you, which you and your husband may have taken out years ago designating each other as beneficiaries, consider whether you need to continue this expense. If you have children, you may want to keep the policies, just be sure to change the beneficiary. But if you do not have children, or they are so well off that there is no need for you to cut into your income in order to provide them with an inheritance that will be less important to them in the future than the premium costs are to you now, then cash in the policy. The purpose of life insurance is to provide financial protection or help to those you love. But if they won't need it, stop paying.

Singles and The Law

So much for the financial aspects of being a smart single. Now we come to the legal ways to secure your future.

Julian S. Perlman, a partner in Summit Rovins & Feldesman of Park Avenue in New York City, points out the importance of contractual arrangements between unmarried people who live together and accumulate assets.

"Societal pressures in law favor marriage. Thus corrections must be made by contract. Since the law only protects married partners, in the case of unmarrieds, contracts can insure what passes to each other in case of separation or death."

If you break up, or one partner dies, how do you establish what goes to whom? With married couples, the law decrees at least one-third to one-half of each other's assets must go to the surviving spouses. But if you elect to remain single and live together, you had better draw up contracts that spell out all details of ownership. You may feel it sounds too coldly businesslike and hate the introduction of a crass note into what has been a happy, emotional and loving relationship. But think of how unhappy you would be if you decided to part ways in a few years and he claimed your piano because he had paid for the tuning and refinishing. Or what if he died and his parents, children or ex-wife tossed you out of the home you and he had shared?

"Unless the assets are in your name as well as his, you need contracts," says Mr. Perlman. Verbal commitments that he will assign income to you are usually not worth the paper they're *not* written on. He may tell you that he wants you to have some of his bonds if he dies, or that he has told his children they are to permit you to continue to live in the house you've both been living in for years until you die at which time the house reverts to his heirs. That's sweet and loving, but not binding. When he dies, chances are they'll have you out on your ear within a week. And the bonds? You gotta be kidding. Unless those promises are spelled out legally, his heirs are bound by their whims rather than his wishes. And no matter how friendly they seemed to be, or how appreciative they were that you cared for him in his final illness, you'll be shocked at how money wipes out memories and all of a sudden you're as welcome as a sinus attack.

The Will

"A will is a 'must' contract to insure that an individual's intent will be carried out as wished and promised," says attorney Perlman.

Nobody expects to die but we all will. That's why it is vital that a couple living together outside the state of matrimony protect each other with wills which clearly spell out who gets what and prevents unintended predators from legally taking what is rightfully and morally yours.

It may sound petty, but every item in a joint domicile should be listed and attributed to one or the other. People's memories are notoriously faulty, consciously or unconsciously and unless you stipulate that the china is yours, the lamps are his, the silverware is yours, etc., you can have a bunch of rampaging relatives pillaging the premises.

Single people need wills. Not only those who live together with a friend or lover, but also single people who live alone. If you are single with children, then of course you will want to provide for them in the event of your death. But even if you do not have children, do you want family members who haven't deserved a phone call in three years to get their hands on the money and possessions you have carefully and lovingly amassed during your lifetime?

The only way you can insure that your assets go to whom and where you want after you die is by making a will.

According to New York State law, and that of many other states as well, property of an unmarried person who dies intestate (without a legal will) passes by statute to the surviving family in the following sequence:

1. Children
2. Parents
3. Brothers and Sisters
4. Nieces and Nephews
5. Grandparents
6. Aunts and Uncles
7. Cousins

Suppose you have an eighty-two-year-old widowed mother who you love dearly and a sister to whom you haven't spoken in seven years, two nephews to whom you tired of sending birthday gifts when they were never acknowledged, and a niece who has the personality of a dead lox and the character of Attila the Hun. If you have no will, your possessions will automatically go to your mother. That seems fine. But remember she is elderly, and when she dies, everything she inherited from you will pass on to your sister and thence to all her darling children. Which means the antique silver you carefully collected and your sister crudely coveted will now be displayed proudly on her sideboard. And the art collection you accumulated will be displayed in the homes of her offspring right along with their paintings on black velvet and sofa-sized pictures of wide-eyed children.

Unless you make out a will to direct the after-her-death flow of your possessions to whomever you deem more deserving, your mother can dispose of your estate however she chooses. All you do is will everything to her in the form of a lifetime trust. Upon her death, your possessions will be distributed as designated in your will. Perhaps you want to establish a scholarship in your name at your alma mater. Or set up a fund for a particular charitable, medical or educational purpose. Your art and silver collections can go to museums, if they are of that calibre. You may want to leave money to friends and friends' children who mean a lot to you. You're too young to die, but then so is everybody. But by making a will now, you will insure that your life's efforts are not wantonly dissipated, and have the satisfaction of knowing that you have left an indelible imprint on the world after you have gone.

Buying a House Together

Suppose you and the man of your choice buy a house together. What's the best way to protect each other's interest in the property should you become separated by intent or death?

"A house could be bought as 'Joint Tenants with Rights of Survivorship' " says Perlman. "In that way, the property automatically goes to the remaining resident when the other dies." If you buy it merely as "Tenants in Common," half of the house automatically belongs to the dead person's heirs, which means you end up sharing ownership of your house with his parents, children or siblings or whoever he has designated in his will as his heirs. They can force the sale if they want the money, or demand an exhorbitant amount for their half.

However, even when the house is purchased as "Joint Tenants with Rights of Survivorship," so that you own the house in full when he dies, and you have each contributed half to the purchase and maintenance, you can get clobbered by inheritance taxes unless you take precautions.

According to Uncle Sam, the first to die is presumed to have put up *all* the money for the house and you can end up having to pay a bundle to the government to get your housemate's half of your house.

"The only way to prove to the IRS that you contributed equally to the house is by keeping careful records of house maintenance," advises Perlman. Your check stubs showing that you paid for the new driveway, the painting, the new deck addition, and so on solidify your position and can cut down or eliminate any inheritance tax.

Even if one person actually did pay more for the house, there's still a way to avoid heavy taxes. Suppose you jointly buy a house for $200,000, and since he has more and makes more, he is happy to put up $150,000 to your $50,000. Just give him a promissory note for $50,000, like he's lending you the money for your share. "How can I repay a $50,000 note?" you shriek. "I can barely cover the cost of manicures now." Worry not, there's a paper gimmick here that gets you off the hook. Everyone is permitted to give a yearly gift of maximum $10,000 to any person without that individual having to claim it as income. So every year, he gives you a little note that says as his annual gift to you, he "forgives" $10,000 of your loan. It's his money, and that's his choice. He repeats that routine yearly and after five years, the $50,000 loan is considered legally repaid and—voila!—you are fully half-owner of the house. Sounds complicated, but it's really simple and could save you a packet.

Rentals: Whose Lease Is It?

Say you two find a great bargain-rental apartment and think you'll have a better chance of getting the place fast if the landlord sees one man's name on the lease rather than a two-named couple. So the lease is issued in your house-mate's name although you pay half the rent each month. Everything goes smoothly for three years at which point the relationship dies and you break up. YOU have to move out. Sure, morally you are just as entitled to the apartment as he is, but legally you're out of luck.

"Make sure that any property you rent has the lease in both your names," warns Perlman.

Social Security Survivor Benefits

You're only thirty-two years old and he's thirty-five, so you are not thinking about social security. But if you're fifty, sixty or seventy and have lived with a man for a number of years retaining your single status out of choice, who gets his social security payments should he die? A wife is automatically entitled to survivor benefits, but who are you, what status do you have?

In the eyes of the law, you could qualify for his social security benefits as a "common-law wife" providing that he does not already have a legal wife. However, many states, such as New York, do not recognize common-law marriages and even if you had lived together for twenty years, upon application to the social security offices in those states you would be told "Forget it, honey. We pay wives only."

If you feel you are entitled to his social security benefits, there is a way. Under the Full Faith and Credit Clause of the United States Constitution, if you have lived as common-law man and wife in any state that recognizes this arrangement as a de facto marriage (such as Pennsylvania) for even one day or night only, you can claim and collect survivor benefits. All you have to do is show a bill for your stay in a Pennsylvania motel where you were registered as Mr. and Mrs. his name. You must also indicate that during your stay, words were exchanged to each other to the effect that you wished to live forever after as husband and wife.

As you can see, there's no question that U.S. laws involving rights, obligations, taxes and inheritance come down heavily in favor of marriage—now. But in the climate of openness that pervades the country today, where some states are recognizing marriages between people of the same sex, changes may soon be effected to correct the inbalanced rights of single people as opposed to married. For the moment, circumlocutions and careful handling of the system are required to achieve parity and knowledge is your best weapon.

❧ TWELVE ❧

You're Not Unmarried . . . You're Single

Words, words, words.
    —WILLIAM SHAKESPEARE, *Hamlet*

SINGLE IS NO LONGER SINGULAR, it's a whole new frame of reference, it's a whole new frame of mind. If being married is becoming no longer the norm, then it stands to reason that being unmarried is no longer the abnorm. So get it out of your head that you are in any way different, or needful of being on the defensive about the fact that you are a single person. Leave that to your mother. But just because she has her mother-of-the-bride dress hanging in the closet is no reason for you to be apologetic for being what you are and choose to be . . . single.

This does not require that you make a public proclamation and get a bumper sticker that says "Single is swell." Being single is not a cause, an occupation, nor even a permanent condition. It is merely the way you choose to live NOW. You may find someone you wish to marry at some point, who knows? But looking for a husband is not your obsessive goal and you should not spend your life in a holding pattern.

In other words, you are not looking, you are living. You are not a woman who is waiting to get married, you are a person who happens to be single.

Free yourself of the compulsion to read those books that tell you how to land a husband and demean you into you feeling like a reject. Ignore those misguided dodoes who ask if you're married yet, which only reveals the real problem is theirs, not yours. Enjoy achievements, your career, your independence and don't let anyone push you into an "until" life which is a throwback to those days when it was a given that a woman worked (at secretarial, typist and other non-executive jobs) *until* she got married. Live your full life happily and serenely as a single person, and if you should happen to come across a man who you think would enrich your life and whom you wish to marry, great. And if you should wish to continue forever as you are, also great.

Women who are between thirty and forty-five are the feminist pioneer generation, the ones who went out there and became everything their mothers and grandmothers for the most part could not. Unfortunately, no one realized that like all pioneers, they would have to face unexpected occurrences for which there was no preparation. The big change in attitudes toward marriage is one of these unanticipated sociological revisions that is a concomitant result of women's new status. It has been left to this group of women to deal with shifting perceptions of the necessity of marriage and the anguish of being the on-the-cusp generation with one foot in the past and one in the future. Brought up in a married society by parents who told them they should go forth and conquer in a man's world but of course, get married and be a mother because that's the real proof of a woman's success, nobody told them that those two goals are potentially antithetical. It's a dirty trick because on one hand we tell them to be proud, and on the other hand to be ashamed.

"I'm successful," says the thirty-six-year-old single woman doctor. "So how come I feel like such a failure?"

But it's changing, and fast. More and more, we are seeing a spate of magazine articles and television programs addressed to the recognition of the respectable state of being single. Public Television had a panel show where the participants stated that the single-without-stigma woman as a viable lifestyle alternative should be made to enter the consciousness of the young so that children learn to perceive single and married as equally normal. It may come to the point where single becomes chic and married women start apologizing for their weakness.

To single women who are suffering through this "must marry" madness, it may seem that the change in societal acceptance is not happening fast enough. But it truly is, and it can be amazing how quickly new codes of mores can become conventional.

Let me point out that in the 1960's it was customary for men to ask only each other what they did for a living. I can still remember being irritated by men's automatically excluding me, an advertising executive, from their conversations because of the implicit assumption that I had nothing to contribute since I was undoubtedly just a cook and diaper changer. Now only twenty years later, a short time for such a major revolution to take effect, women are asked "And what do you do?" as a matter of course.

Unfortunately, this question has thrown housewives into a state of defensiveness which is as unfair as the old consignment to the kitchen was to career women. *No woman should be self-conscious about announcing herself to be whatever she has chosen to be.* If the 1980's and nineties are to have any epithet, it should be "The Era of Choices." Married or single, career woman or homemaker, all are socially endorsed alternative lifestyles today.

There is no longer any need for apologias, explanations, self-doubts or sadness because you are *not* something that others expect you to be. If you have found that so far you like living as a single person, if you decide to have a child and be a single mother, these are your choices and may not be judged by the way others have opted to live. Look around you and listen. There is no longer any better or worse, aberrant or normal. It is the time to accept yourself happily for what and who you are and not identify yourself by what you are not. You may be married, or you may be single. Who cares? It's just a statistic, not a life sentence.

We have become aware of how mere words and terminologies can affect the way we actually think about people and issues. The switch from the old titles of "Miss" and "Mrs." which had caused society to view single women as different than married, to the now universally acceptable "Ms." has altered public perceptions tremendously. Don't allow words to influence your state of mind and sense of pride and self. You are NOT not married . . . you are single. So what else is happening?